Praise for
Building Corporate Soul

"*Building Corporate Soul* shows how twenty-first-century leaders can transform their companies into inspired communities."

—Adrian Hallmark, Chairman and CEO, Bentley Motors

"Culture is everything—*Building Corporate Soul* provides an actionable framework to build a culture at the workplace that is both human centric and success driven."

—Aaron Hurst, CEO, Imperative and
author of *The Purpose Economy*

"Ralf Specht brings together practitioner realism with the theory of an academic into a new framework for building corporate soul. Never has there been a time more important for corporations to take note; as the boundaries between personal and professional, human and business, purpose and profit become less defined. *Building Corporate Soul* is a trusted guide for this journey."

—Charles Trevail, CEO, Interbrand

"Trust is the engine oil for high-performance teams—and this book provides a framework which makes this actionable and measurable. What this book contains is the holy grail of companies today: how to build and sustain a human-centric performance culture. It's exactly what's needed in organizations everywhere right now."

—Greg McKeown, Author of *The New York Times*
best sellers *Effortless* and *Essentialism*

"In sports, teams with soul win. In business, companies with soul succeed. This book connects the critical dots and provides an actionable framework that could help turn a company into a powerhouse."

—Brett Gosper, Head of NFL Europe and UK
and former CEO, World Rugby

"With *Building Corporate Soul*, Ralf plumbs the depths of what really matters, and in doing so, completely redefines what it means to chart a course for an organization. A must-have guide for plotting a true north star."

—Kevin Allen, Founder of E. I. Games Corporation and
author of the *Wall Street Journal* best seller *The Hidden Agenda*

"We've come a long way since Milton Friedman indoctrinated company leadership to myopically focus on maximizing shareholder value. But the world has changed in the past 50 years, and now *Building Corporate Soul* pinpoints what today's employees crave, what managers have been missing, and what shareholders didn't realize they needed all along."

—Les Trachtman, Author of *Don't F**k It Up*, serial entrepreneur, and
adjunct instructor, Johns Hopkins Carey School of Business

"We are on the verge of a new way of defining the way we do business and design organizational cultures. *Building Corporate Soul* shows in many case studies that the shared purpose of a company is the nucleus for this change. Soul-searching for businesses does make sense."

—Michael Alberg-Seberich, Managing Partner,
Wider Sense, Berlin, and co-author of the 2020
book *The Corporate Social Mind*

"*Building Corporate Soul* reflects my experience of working with successful entrepreneurs for many years: A strong passion for products and services on the basis of a belief system that is real and authentic is critical. What Ralf calls 'shared behavior' and 'shared understanding' are the cornerstones to a fully engaged workforce with clear entrepreneurial direction. This is the future of business!"

—Shalini Khemka, Founder and Chief Executive, E2E and
Business Advisory Board Member to the Mayor of London

POWERING CULTURE & SUCCESS WITH THE **SOUL SYSTEM**™

BUILDING
CORPORATE
SOUL

RALF SPECHT

FAST
COMPANY
Press

Fast Company Press
New York, New York
www.fastcompanypress.com

This work is being published under the Fast Company Press imprint by an exclusive arrangement with Fast Company. Fast Company and the Fast Company logo are registered trademarks of Mansueto Ventures, LLC. The Fast Company Press logo is a wholly owned trademark of Mansueto Ventures, LLC.

Distributed by Greenleaf Book Group

For ordering information or special discounts for bulk purchases, please contact Greenleaf Book Group at PO Box 91869, Austin, TX 78709, 512.891.6100.

Design and composition by Greenleaf Book Group
Cover design by Greenleaf Book Group
Cover concept by Jack Bleakley
For permissions credits, please see page 252-253, which is a continuation of the copyright page.

Publisher's Cataloging-in-Publication data is available.

Print ISBN: 978-1-63908-002-1

eBook ISBN: 978-1-63908-003-8

Part of the Tree Neutral® program, which offsets the number of trees consumed in the production and printing of this book by taking proactive steps, such as planting trees in direct proportion to the number of trees used: www.treeneutral.com

TreeNeutral®

Printed in the United States of America on acid-free paper

21 22 23 24 25 26 27   10 9 8 7 6 5 4 3 2 1

First Edition

I am dedicating this book

to leaders around the world

who share my vision of

making soulless companies a thing of the past.

The companies that survive longest are the ones
that work out what they uniquely can give to the world—
not just growth or money but their excellence,
their respect for others,
or their ability to make people happy.
Some call those things a soul.

Charles Handy
social philosopher

Contents

Foreword

Nearly twenty years ago, in the fledgling days of The Cassie Partnership (TCP), I was advised by a leading academic in my new field of "organizational behavior" as follows: "It is clear that TCP's work in aligning behavior with purpose is five years ahead of its time. Congratulations. Unfortunately for you, most CEOs have not yet woken up to the fact that their world has irrevocably changed in your direction . . . but eventually they will. Good luck." I did not know whether to laugh or cry.

Shortly after this meeting, however, I was introduced to the CEO of one of the world's leading credit card companies. My "luck" was that he was embarking on a "people first" transformation program and sought a like-minded thinker able to drive—and sustain—the innovative behaviors that lead to success. So, my advisor was correct, and CEOs did "wake up." What is telling is that without exception the leaders TCP has enjoyed working with across categories from finance to media to IT consulting over the past twenty years have been visionaries. These inspirational people were not only awake but also instinctively anticipated the winds of transformational change.

Most recently, one of these inspirational leaders was Ralf Specht, the author of *Building Corporate Soul.* The reason I opened with the story of the academic is that I believe Ralf is similarly five years ahead of his contemporaries. *Building Corporate Soul* is not a philosophy plucked from thin air. It is a philosophy hewn from frontline leadership experience with the added benefit of being practical, applicable, actionable, and measurable now, immediately.

In these unprecedented times, leaders cannot afford to wait five minutes, never mind five years. They cannot hide behind change programs that everyone knows will change nothing. They must take leaps, taking their people on audacious, purpose-led journeys that transform the value of the company to all stakeholders. They must integrate ESG principles into their corporate behavior and do so not as a checkbox exercise but while encouraging their business to fly, to reimagine. The objective of Ralf's book is to impart the inspiration, wisdom, and learnings from having built a company—designed at birth to challenge traditional category business models—from concept to global presence, with well over 1,200 employees in 18 countries, in only a few years.

His book provides a brilliant framework—The Soul System™—that allows leaders to act immediately for the long-term benefit of their business. The Soul System™ gives answers on how to approach this seismic shift by giving away practical and reality-tested approaches that enable leaders to maximize the impact of their workforce. In so doing they will gain the broad acceptance of society as a whole—winning the hearts of their stakeholders on an emotional level and convincing their minds on a rational basis.

Building Corporate Soul is, in short, the means by which leaders can inspire their people to do what they did not believe possible. My firsthand observation of the author reveals, however, that this is no elixir, no magic potion. Ralf Specht may well be too modest, too generous of spirit to say this, but to build corporate soul takes *courage*—not simply the courage of one's convictions, but the courage to challenge the conventions of how to create value sustainably in these extraordinary times.

Ralf has, in this book, provided the vision *and* the pathway. It is a true practitioner's guide with proven steps to building corporate soul. You, however, dear leader, have to grasp what is inside you in order to unlock the value within these covers. You have to ask yourself, "Why am I here?"—so that your personal purpose can align with that of your company's.

And then you have to be the first to have the courage to do what you did not believe you were capable of.

Neil Cassie
Founder of The Cassie Partnership

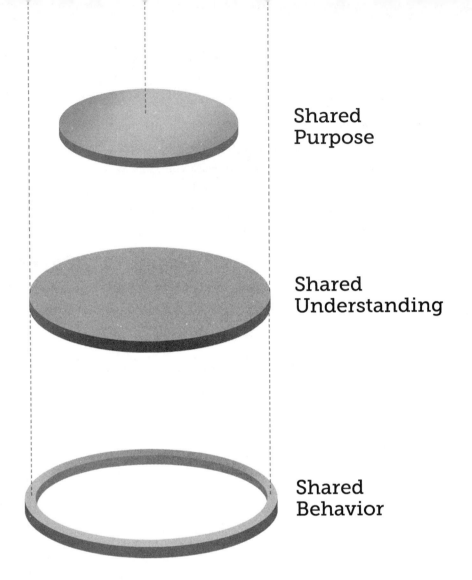

Shared
Purpose

Shared
Understanding

Shared
Behavior

The Soul System™

The Time Is Now

Times of change show one's real character. It was no different when my sudden departure from Spark44, an industry-first global marketing agency joint venture with Jaguar Land Rover, was communicated to the 1,200 staff we had globally. I was the last man standing of the founding partners. Many members of my team got in touch to share their sadness and speak about the impact they felt I had made on their lives. The emails and messages I received deeply moved me and inspired me to write this book. Their statements made me realize the legacy that had been created—a unique global intercultural force of dedicated professionals who shared a common purpose and were driven to deliver. Outsiders might have thought creating a company from scratch with 19 offices and 1,200 people and $100+ million in revenue was the legacy. Insiders knew it was the way we worked together and created a new approach to how advertising agencies could collaborate across continents and cultures and create globally effective work in the most efficient way.

I had always felt that I had a good relationship with my teams, but there was something in these messages that went beyond what you call a good relationship. That something was a deeper and more meaningful expression of what it had meant to be part of the team—the family—we had created. It did prove that what we had built was on a substantially higher level than what is the norm. We had been able to win our people's hearts. We had been able to convince their minds. We had been able to build a company with a unique spirit. We had been able to create *corporate soul*.

For me, this was simply the way it had to be done. It wasn't something to contemplate again and again. But whenever I talked to others about how we were operating, I learned that this wasn't the norm. One day, I shared this observation with my personal coach, Katharina Thünnihsen. She has been in the business of coaching corporations for decades and has seen the opposite far too often. "I am dealing with so many companies that would die for a corporate spirit like that which comes through all of these messages," she told me. And she encouraged me to write up how we did it.

The more I looked into this topic, the more inspiring and thought-provoking cases I found. The ancient Greek philosopher Aristotle said, "A soul is the actuality of a body that has life," where life means the capacity for self-sustenance, growth, and reproduction. These three dimensions are relevant for living species—and for corporations alike. Interestingly, the connection between *soul* and corporations has been made more often in a negative sense than in a positive one. Roland Marchand's book *Creating the Corporate Soul*,[1] published in 1998, refers to the legal positions at the turn of the nineteenth and twentieth centuries when US courts had to deal with a significant number of cases in which the term *soul* was used overtly: "The vulnerability of the new corporate giants to charges of soullessness emerged again and again in the titles of their wounded rebuttals: 'The Heart of a "Soulless Corporation"' (1908), 'Corporations and Souls' (1912), 'United States Steel: A Corporation with a Soul' (1921), 'Puts Flesh and Blood into "Soulless Corporation"'

- - - - - - - - - - -

1   Roland Marchand. *Creating the Corporate Soul: The Rise of Public Relations and Corporate Imagery in American Big Business*. Berkeley: University of California Press, 1998.

(1921), 'Refuting the Old Idea of the Soulless Corporations' (1926), and 'Humanizing a "Soulless Corporation"' (1937)."

Building Corporate Soul is not looking at the absence of soul. It celebrates companies that have been successful at building—or in some cases rebuilding—it. At a time when *purpose* seems to be the flavor of the day in discussions about corporate leadership, this book aims to provide a framework for how to take purpose to a higher level: *corporate soul.* If you are able to build *corporate soul,* the rewards to your company are huge. Corporations in many sectors and cultures are taking every effort to achieve it—at every level and every day. They are united in how they ensure a solid *understanding* of the company's direction and how they leverage key principles of *behavior* that make a difference for the thousands of people who give their very best for "their" company day in and day out.

The Soul Index

As I began looking at which companies have already built their unique corporate soul, I started noticing an important common thread: performance. In particular, I noticed that having corporate soul affected a company's performance for the better, it seemed. But I wanted to quantify this correlation/connection—to prove with hard data that having corporate soul not only provides meaningful social benefits but also a benefit to the bottom line. That led to the creation of the Soul Index.

The Soul Index is a global ranking that identifies companies across a wide range of sectors that have corporate soul. In researching the quantitative studies available that identify the performance of companies in terms of their brand strength, their brand impact, their employer brand qualities, and their ability to create employee satisfaction, a correlation emerged between the business success and the level of employee engagement and satisfaction and their appreciation for their company's CEO. The companies listed on the Soul Index speak the language of success based on a clear system of the key elements of the Soul System™: a *shared understanding* (vision, mission, values, and spirit) and corresponding *shared behaviors* (leadership, ecosystem, drivers, compensation, recruitment, development, partnerships, and followers) centered on a *shared purpose* allowing their associates to experience a workplace where people are leading people to achieve what they did not believe possible.

The cumulative performance of the portfolio of the top twenty companies in the Soul Index speaks for itself:

Cumulative Performance	5 Years (2016-2020)	3 Years (2018-2020)	1 Year (2020)
Soul Index	199.44%	92.13%	26.16%
Nasdaq	180.59%	101.49%	47.58%
S&P 500	83.77%	40.49%	16.26%
Dow Jones	75.65%	23.82%	7.25%

The Soul Index

1. Adobe
2. Salesforce
3. Microsoft
4. Stryker
5. Cisco
6. ULTIMATE SOFTWARE
7. Deloitte
8. Amazon
9. Workday
10. Hilton
11. Apple
12. SAP
13. Google
14. American Express
15. IKEA
16. Oracle
17. Southwest Airlines
18. Adidas
19. Intel
20. Costco Wholesale

These results are a testament of the value that companies with corporate soul are able to build compared to their peers. In fact, they demonstrate that the leadership behaviors that build soul are synonymous with the behaviors that build success. If one looks at the distribution of categories, it becomes obvious that tech companies own the lion's share of the top twenty ranking. The majority of companies operate in the area of IT, tech, and software. We'll see how the category structure evolves in the future.

The 2021 Soul Index is included here so you can see the caliber of companies that have made the list. Three of the Soul Index's top thirty companies are featured in this book. Salesforce, Hilton, and IKEA have all been very proactive in defining their shared purpose and have created a shared understanding and shared behaviors to ensure that the company is providing an equally successful experience for customers and employees alike while establishing holistic relationships with their stakeholders across all areas.

When you visit www.buildingcorporatesoul.com, you will always find the most up-to-date ranking of the best-performing companies when it comes to building corporate soul.

As the Soul Index proves, making the effort to build and maintain corporate soul provides significant value and growth. So how can a company find and build its corporate soul? And then how does a company ensure its soul grows and thrives?

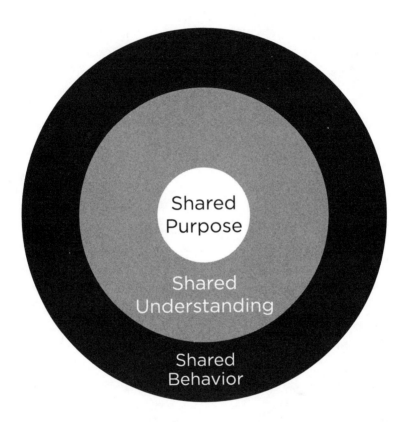

Figure 1: The three dimensions of the Soul System™.

CHAPTER 1

The Corporate Soul

Understanding and behavior are the two sides of the coin that allow corporations to establish and nurture their soul.

Chapter Goal:

- - - - - - - - - - - - - -

Understand the critical dimensions
to building corporate soul.

"*I am the master of my fate; I am the captain of my soul.*" William Ernest Henley's famous line from his poem "Invictus" provided inspiration and energy to Nelson Mandela during his twenty-seven years in prison. Mandela read it again and again to remind himself that it was he who was the "captain of [his] soul." It helped him to understand that it was up to him to frame his perception of himself, inside and out.

What is true for individuals is also true for corporations. Their leadership teams are the masters of their fate; they are the captains of the soul of their enterprises. But what do they need to embrace to drive that soul for the best of their enterprise and all of their stakeholders? There is no answer to this question without clarity of purpose. Being clear about your business's purpose is the foundation for it to develop, build, and grow its corporate soul.

What Is Corporate Soul?

From my experience of working *in* a few companies and *for* quite a few companies and brands, I strongly believe that corporate soul is the ultimate currency of success. It is a function of aligning both corporate understanding and behavior around a purpose that is inclusive to all stakeholders—by "simply" ensuring that all three levels are a *shared* property of the firm and its people.

> If corporations *walk the talk*—meaning that they *behave* on the basis of shared understanding—then you find companies with soul.

That shared purpose allows a company to develop a *shared understanding* of what drives that company and its people, as well as the corresponding shared behaviors that reflect that shared understanding.

As a result, shared understanding and shared behaviors are inextricably linked in building the soul of a company and its brand. If corporations *walk the talk*—meaning that they *behave* on the basis of shared understanding—then you find companies with soul. As the social philosopher Charles Handy said, "The companies that survive longest are the ones that work out what they uniquely can give to the world, not just growth or money but their excellence, their respect for others, or their ability to make people happy. Some call those things a soul." This was a new perspective that Handy introduced in his 1989 book *The Age of Unreason*.[2] Until then, a different view had been predominant in the world of business. Handy, who has been rated among the Thinkers50, a

---

2   Charles Handy. *The Age of Unreason*. Boston: Harvard Business School Press, 1990.

private list of the most influential living management thinkers, was one of the first who understood that soul might also be a relevant attribute when it comes to corporations.

In September 1970, Milton Friedman wrote about shareholder value in *The New York Times Magazine* in an article titled "The Social Responsibility of Business Is to Increase Its Profits." In 1997, the Business Roundtable[3] (an influential thinktank of two hundred CEOs from the largest and most influential companies in the United States) formalized the Friedman approach with this definition of corporate purpose: "The paramount duty of management and of boards of directors is to the corporation's stockholders. The interests of other stakeholders are relevant as a derivative of the duty to stockholders." It wasn't until 2011 that this perspective began to change. That year, Michael E. Porter and Mark R. Kramer published their article "Creating Shared Value: How to Reinvent Capitalism—and Unleash a Wave of Innovation and Growth."[4] It was an academic perspective coming a few years after the 2008 financial crisis, but it created the basis for what was to come.

Fast-forward to 2018 when Larry Fink, CEO of the world's largest asset managing company BlackRock, first introduced the concept of Purpose in his annual letter to CEOs. In 2019, he reinforced his position when he wrote[5] to CEOs again. This time, it got him headlines in the business press all over the world: "Purpose is not the sole pursuit of profits but the animating force for achieving them. Profits are in no way inconsistent with purpose—in fact, profits and purpose are inextricably linked. Profits are essential if a company is to effectively serve all of its stakeholders over time—not only shareholders, but also employees, customers, and communities. Similarly, when a company truly understands and expresses

- - - - - - - - - - -

3   http://www.ralphgomory.com/wp-content/uploads/2018/05/Business-Roundtable-1997.
     pdf

4   https://hbr.org/2011/01/the-big-idea-creating-shared-value

5   https://www.blackrock.com/americas-offshore/en/2019-larry-fink-ceo-letter

its purpose, it functions with the focus and strategic discipline that drive long-term profitability. Purpose unifies management, employees, and communities. It drives ethical behavior and creates an essential check on actions that go against the best interests of stakeholders. Purpose guides culture, provides a framework for consistent decision-making, and, ultimately, helps sustain long-term financial returns for the shareholders of your company. The World Needs Your Leadership.'"

Fink would not have made purpose the key element of his letter if he were not completely convinced that it was the right path. The fact that he was convinced was no real surprise—because he is a member of the Business Roundtable. When this group revisited the topic on August 19, 2019, they came to a different conclusion compared to the one in 1997. They prioritized creating value for customers; investing in employees; fostering diversity and inclusion; dealing fairly and ethically with suppliers; supporting the communities in which they work; and protecting the environment over prioritizing the corporate stockholders. Alex Gorsky, board chairman and CEO of Johnson & Johnson and chair of the Business Roundtable Corporate Governance Committee, summarized at the time, "This new statement better reflects the way corporations can and should operate today. It affirms the essential role corporations can play in improving our society when CEOs are truly committed to meeting the needs of all stakeholders."[6]

Statement on the Purpose of a Corporation[7]
Published by the Business Roundtable, August 19, 2019

Americans deserve an economy that allows each person to succeed through hard work and creativity and to lead a life of meaning and dignity. We believe the free-market system is the

----

6   https://www.businessroundtable.org/business-roundtable-redefines-the-purpose-of-a-corporation-to-promote-an-economy-that-serves-all-americans

7   https://opportunity.businessroundtable.org/ourcommitment/

best means of generating good jobs, a strong and sustainable economy, innovation, a healthy environment, and economic opportunity for all.

Businesses play a vital role in the economy by creating jobs, fostering innovation, and providing essential goods and services.

Businesses make and sell consumer products; manufacture equipment and vehicles; support the national defense; grow and produce food; provide health care; generate and deliver energy; and offer financial, communications, and other services that underpin economic growth.

While each of our individual companies serves its own corporate purpose, we share a fundamental commitment to all of our stakeholders. We commit to:

Delivering value to our customers. We will further the tradition of American companies leading the way in meeting or exceeding customer expectations.

Investing in our employees. This starts with compensating them fairly and providing important benefits. It also includes supporting them through training and education that help develop new skills for a rapidly changing world. We foster diversity and inclusion, dignity, and respect.

Dealing fairly and ethically with our suppliers. We are dedicated to serving as good partners to the other companies, large and small, that help us meet our missions.

Supporting the communities in which we work. We respect the people in our communities and protect the environment by embracing sustainable practices across our businesses.

Generating long-term value for shareholders who provide the capital that allows companies to invest, grow, and innovate. We are committed to transparency and effective engagement with shareholders.

> Each of our stakeholders is essential. We commit to deliver
> value to all of them, for the future success of our companies,
> our communities, and our country.

What a change—with this influential group of leaders it becomes very likely that we will see change happening in the right direction. When you compare the two concepts the obvious question is not "if" the stakeholders are being considered (as they are as well considered in the shareholder-value approach), but "how" they are being considered.

In 2020, Ernst & Young (EY) sponsored a survey of 474 global executives conducted by Harvard Business Review Analytical Services. The resulting report, called "The Business Case for Purpose,"[8] provided very clear results, stating that "there is near-unanimity in the business community about the value of purpose in driving performance."

But is everybody walking the talk? Apparently not. The survey results went on to say, "Less than half of the executives surveyed said their company had actually articulated a strong sense of purpose and used it as a way to make decisions and strengthen motivation."

It gets worse. EY concludes from the data that "only a few companies appear to have embedded their purpose to a point where they have reaped its full potential." It is fair to say that only a shared purpose can become an embedded purpose.

One company, however, that understands the importance of shared purpose is Unilever. In the spring of 2020, Unilever's CEO Alan Jope gave a remarkable response in an interview with *Bloomberg Businessweek* in the context of the COVID-19 pandemic outbreak. Jope was asked how he navigated between profits and doing the right thing, given the current circumstances.

----

8   https://assets.ey.com/content/dam/ey-sites/ey-com/en_gl/topics/digital/ey-the-business-case-for-purpose.pdf

He responded, "I think if you frame the recovery as economy vs. health, it's a false framing. In the same way, we shouldn't talk about purpose over profits. And I really hate to set up some trade-off on purpose vs. profits."[9] His words demonstrate real leadership in action:

- positioning the various brands on doing real good

- making sustainability a key element of Unilever's supply chain

- pushing the firm's policies in the area of being a responsible employer

Unilever is one of the companies in the Firms of Endearment[10] Index that professors Raj Sisodia and Jag Sheth, as well as customer behavior expert David B. Wolfe, have created. They assess performances of companies that fit defined criteria based on qualitative metrics, such as companies that subscribe to a purpose that is different from and beyond making money and actively aligns with the interests of all stakeholder groups. Their analysis drew an antipode to the *Good to Great* approach from Jim Collins,[11] which focused on a company's financial characteristics. Their view: "Today's greatest companies are fueled by passion and purpose, not cash. They earn large profits by helping all their stakeholders thrive: customers, investors, employees, partners, communities, and society. These rare, authentic firms of endearment act in powerfully positive ways that stakeholders recognize, value, admire, and even love."[12] What really supports their point is the performance that these companies have been able to deliver.

----

9   https://www.bloomberg.com/news/features/2020-05-12/unilever-ceo-on-coronavirus-pandemic-purpose-led-businesses

10   The Firms of Endearment featured in the book have outperformed the S&P 500 by fourteen times and Good to Great Companies by six times over a period of fifteen years.

11   Jim Collins. *Good to Great.* New York: HarperCollins, 2001.

12   https://www.firmsofendearment.com

Comparing the Firms of Endearment indices (US and International) to the S&P 500 and the Good to Great Index, the outperformance is mind-blowing.

Cumulative Performance	15 Years	10 Years	5 Years	3 Years
US Firms of Endearment	1.681%	410%	151%	83%
Int'l Firms of Endearment	1.180%	512%	154%	47%
Good to Great Companies	263%	176%	158%	222%
S&P 500	118%	107%	61%	57%

Table 1: Comparative cumulative performance of Firms of Endearment.

It is fair to say that the companies that can carry the Firms of Endearment badge are those that are clear about their purpose and provide a shared understanding and shared behaviors across their workforce on their way to building corporate soul. Again, it is a similar pattern as we have seen with the Soul Index, where the gap between the S&P 500 and the Soul Index on a 5-year basis has been 115.67 percentage points—with the Firms of Endearment it has been 90 percentage points (US firms) and 93 percentage points (Int'l).

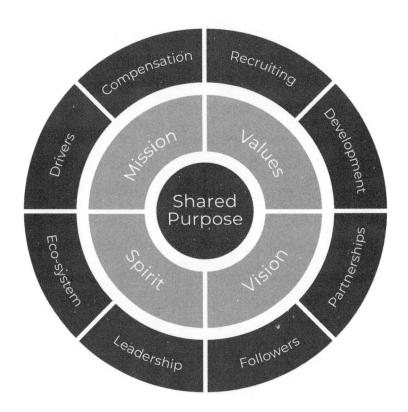

Figure 2: The components of shared understanding and shared
behaviors surrounding the shared purpose.

CHAPTER 2

The Soul System™

A shared understanding of what a company's purpose means and the corresponding shared behaviors across the company are critical for allowing the corporate soul to emerge.

Chapter Goal:

Understand/internalize that *shared* is the magic word that allows a company to truly build corporate soul.

"If you cannot measure it, you cannot manage it." Everybody attributes this saying to management thinker Peter Drucker, but he actually never said it. Put that aside, though, as the saying has its merits in the context of the Soul System™.

The Soul System™ is a framework that enables business leaders to assess the level of corporate soul that their firm has. The shared aspect of the three dimensions of the Soul System™ allows companies to measure their achieved levels of understanding and behavior on the basis of the firm's purpose across all areas of the business—internationally or domestically, across different departments or across different leadership levels.

To develop corporate soul, making a shared purpose the guiding principle for the entire company is critical. You accomplish that by defining the different elements of the Soul System™ for your company. At the core of the Soul System™ sits that all-important shared purpose—it represents the heart of everything your company does. Surrounding that core are four key elements—*vision, mission, values,* and *spirit*—that build shared understanding. The next dimension consists of eight aspects of shared behaviors, which we'll cover in subsequent chapters.

> To develop corporate soul, making a shared purpose the guiding principle for the entire company is critical.

Creating the Soul System™ is not just a task for top management. It is a company-wide project that never ends. It is not a straight line. Even the companies that do extremely well in this space have lost their way at times. In start-ups this can happen when the founding generation leaves. In established companies, management changes often include the risk of losing the way. Few companies recognize that they have lost their soul—and then they start to look at it as a detour on their way forward. They find a contemporary way to give the soul back to their company, which often allows them to make giant leaps in business success during the next few years. Companies that implement the Soul System™ methodology and create "their" Soul System™ all have one thing in common: a shared understanding of the forces that drive their success and the shared behaviors that express that understanding. And they all are ready to be on the journey for the long haul.

Shared is the magic word of the Soul System™. A shared understanding and shared behaviors allow the company to get to the higher level. As I mentioned earlier, one level out from the shared purpose core of the Soul System™ are the four most critical parameters—vision, mission, values, and spirit—but these terms are often mixed up by businesses. Clarity is key, so companies need to ask the following questions to establish clear definitions: What is the vision? What is the mission? Which values are at play? Which spirit is desired? And these questions need to be answered in a way that everybody inside the organization fully understands.

> *Shared* is the magic word of the Soul System™.

Vision, Mission, Values

Let's start with vision. In the truest sense of the word, a vision is created by a visionary. Whether it is the founder or the founding team in the early days of the company, or the board as the company progresses—it is the leaders at the top of the organization who work out the *vision statement* that expresses what the organization wants to be for the foreseeable future. It provides direction for where senior management sees the future of the company.

LinkedIn is a good example of this. When you look at its vision statement, it is pretty clear: "Create economic opportunity for every member of the global workforce."[13]

Based on that clarity of thought, it is time to define the mission and to work out a clear *mission statement*. This is the moment when it needs to be made crystal clear what business the company is in. Make no mistake, this is not about the category the company is operating in. In the case of LinkedIn, you do not find any reference to the category of social media in its mission statement. Instead, you get a very clear sense of what the company offers its customers and what it does on a day-to-day basis (products, services, and innovation) in order to ultimately achieve its vision: "Connect the world's professionals to make them more productive and successful."[14]

Values are a description of the desired organizational culture. When vision serves as the North Star and mission as the compass, values are supposed to become the navigation points for the organization to understand

----

13, 14   https://about.linkedin.com/

both with their hearts and minds how one ideally behaves within the company. In LinkedIn's case, these values[15] are—again—very simple and clear and easy for everyone to understand.

1. Members first

2. Relationships matter

3. Be open, honest, and constructive

4. Inspire excellence

5. Take intelligent risks

6. Act like an owner of #OneLinkedIn

They are a combination of outward focus and inward attitudes that are supposed to characterize life at LinkedIn.

The sense of clarity that they provide is mirrored when you look at how employees relate to their company.[16] Eighty-seven percent of their staff are proud to be part of LinkedIn, and 78 percent are motivated by the company's vision, mission, and values. For 72 percent, the company's mission was important when they were looking for a new job. And the number one reason why employees stay at LinkedIn is its company mission.

One of the many issues people face when building that logic for their own company is that purpose, vision, and mission often get confused. But they are not the same. In short, purpose declares why the company exists, vision defines the desired future state, and mission expresses the direction that is required to make the purpose become real and for the vision to manifest itself in the marketplace.

Let's look at LinkedIn again. Its mission is to "connect the world's

----

15   https://careers.linkedin.com/culture-and-values

16   https://www.comparably.com/companies/linkedin/mission

professionals to make them more productive and successful." The mission offers clear benefits (*more productive and successful*), whereas the purpose states what LinkedIn does on a much broader basis. Their purpose is simply *to facilitate professional networking.*

As the Soul Index has shown, tech companies seem to be in a good place when it comes to building their corporate soul, as 60% of the top 20 companies belong to that category. But there are great examples also outside tech. Johnson & Johnson is particularly interesting. Here´s why: A long time before the discussion about the importance of purpose hit the executive management literature, Robert Wood Johnson[17], J&J´s former chairman (1932–1963) crafted the firm´s credo back in 1943. Reading it today, one has to think, "Why did it take the business roundtable so long to move to a stakeholder approach?" (as mentioned in chapter 1). Even more than 75 years later, it reads like a blueprint for the stakeholder concept:

> We believe our first responsibility is to the patients, doctors and nurses, to mothers and fathers and all others who use our products and services. In meeting their needs everything we do must be of high quality. We must constantly strive to provide value, reduce our costs and maintain reasonable prices. Customers' orders must be serviced promptly and accurately. Our business partners must have an opportunity to make a fair profit.
>
> We are responsible to our employees who work with us throughout the world. We must provide an inclusive work environment where each person must be considered as an individual. We must respect their diversity and dignity and recognize their merit. They must have a sense of security,

---

17 https://www.jnj.com/latest-news/johnson-johnson-ceo-alex-gorsky-reflects-on-the-power-of-the-companys-credo

fulfillment and purpose in their jobs. Compensation must be fair and adequate and working conditions clean, orderly and safe. We must support the health and well-being of our employees and help them fulfill their family and other personal responsibilities. Employees must feel free to make suggestions and complaints. There must be equal opportunity for employment, development and advancement for those qualified. We must provide highly capable leaders and their actions must be just and ethical.

We are responsible to the communities in which we live and work and to the world community as well. We must help people be healthier by supporting better access and care in more places around the world. We must be good citizens —support good works and charities, better health and education, and bear our fair share of taxes. We must maintain in good order the property we are privileged to use, protecting the environment and natural resources.

Our final responsibility is to our stockholders. Business must make a sound profit. We must experiment with new ideas. Research must be carried on, innovative programs developed, investments made for the future and mistakes paid for. New equipment must be purchased, new facilities provided and new products launched. Reserves must be created to provide for adverse times. When we operate according to these principles, the stockholders should realize a fair return.

Over the years, that credo has been updated but always kept its initial principles. Whether it has been the addition of "protecting the environment and natural resources" in 1979 or the addition of the word "fathers" to recognize male responsibility in growing families. Equality works both ways, doesn´t it? When the 75th birthday of the credo was celebrated, it was updated once again reflecting the importance of diversity, inclusion, and sense of purpose for the employees.

While the credo consists of 341 words and is everything but a short and snappy summary of what matters at J&J, it actually complements their statements for purpose, vision, and mission that follow the current management language. J&J's purpose is to "blend heart, science and ingenuity to change the trajectory of health for humanity," which is a great springboard for the company's vision statement: "to help people see better, connect better, live better." Their mission statement references the credo as the belief system for everything the company does: "*Our Credo Stems from a Belief that Consumers, Employees and the Community Are All Equally Important.*"

The leaders of both companies—LinkedIn and Johnson & Johnson—have received consistently high Glassdoor CEO[18] approval ratings. While LinkedIn's Jeff Weiner even achieved a 100% rating once (2014), both leaders have been high up in the ranking with 97% rankings for Jeff Weiner in 2018 and 2021, and 95% rankings for Alex Gorsky. Both leaders published very personal farewell messages on social media when they announced their moves to step down as CEO and move into the chairman position. Alex Gorsky's note[19] is special:

> In the days since the announcement that I will be transitioning out of the role of CEO of Johnson & Johnson at the end of this year, the flood of emails and other messages I have received from so many of you has been truly humbling. I spent this weekend sharing them with my wife, Pat, my son, Nick, and his new fiancée, Haley, and words cannot express just how moving it has been for us to experience such an outpouring of love and support.

----

18   https://www.glassdoor.com/Award/Highest-Rated-CEOs-2017-LST

19   https://www.linkedin.com/pulse/reflections-gratitude-alex-gorsky

Until last week, I would have said that the hardest decision I've faced in life was my choice to leave the military and pursue a new career in the private sector. I had always been drawn to healthcare, but still worried that I couldn't possibly find the same exhilarating unity of purpose that had characterized my six years as a soldier in the U.S. Army.

However, when I showed up to interview for an entry-level job as a sales rep at Janssen back in 1988, the first question I was asked was about Our Credo—that living document that would go on to guide me through times of both triumph and crisis for more than three decades. I had found my next mission, and I know now that I couldn't have asked for a better opportunity to make an impact on the world than the work we do together at Johnson & Johnson on behalf of all our stakeholders.

Serving as your CEO for nearly ten years has been the great honor of my life, and never more so than in the past 18 months. Living and working through a global pandemic has required bold action in the face of uncertainty, called on each of us to reassess our priorities, and made it crystal clear that every single thing we hold most dear in life is built on a foundation of good health.

These lessons imparted by the pandemic go far beyond business for me. You see, as COVID-19 was first sweeping through the world in late 2019 and early 2020, I was simultaneously dealing with challenges in my personal life, including the sudden death of my father, the diagnosis of a significant health issue for a family member, and the loss of my longtime head of security to COVID-19.

I know that I am not alone when I say that the last year and a half has given me both a new understanding and a new appreciation of what matters most in life. Even when faced with struggles of their own, my family never stopped being a source of great strength and inspiration for me as all of us at Johnson & Johnson worked to safeguard families around the world with our portfolio of lifesaving medicines and health solutions, while also racing to develop our Janssen COVID-19 vaccine.

I owe a particular debt of gratitude to Pat for her constant support. Without my wife's grace, generosity, and wisdom, I don't know that I could have shown up as the leader my company needed during these extraordinary times.

So, while my decision to transition to a new role wasn't an easy one to make, I know this is the right call. It's time for me to spend more time with the family I love so very much and welcome this new chapter of my life as Executive Chairman. Beginning January 3, 2022, I can do so with total confidence that my Johnson & Johnson family is in good hands with Joaquin Duato as our new Chief Executive Officer.

This farewell message titled "Reflection and Gratitude" is a very personal statement coming straight from the heart. The photo that shows him and his wife complements the personal touch of the message. This authentic way of communication is reflected back in the comments of employees. The tone of the often very personal and warm comments from J&J employees reminded me of the messages I received upon stepping down as CEO. One comment from an ex-colleague of Gorsky summarized it perfectly:

So many memories as a J&J alumn and somebody that will always have the J&J shirt on. Thanks to the opportunities I was given during my 20 years at this great corporation I can do what I am doing now. (. . .) Your humbleness and the care you showed about people left a mark in my professional life.

Hope we can see each other again. Wish you continue happiness and I admire what you have decided. You have the clear picture of what matters in life."

It comes as no surprise that the company can be consistently found on Glassdoor's Best Places to Work rankings, but also on more specific areas such as "Best Workplaces to Grow Your Career" or Fast Company's "Best Workplace for Innovators."[20] J&J operates in three market segments of the human healthcare market and is used to taking a holistic view on the entire spectrum from prevention, diagnosis, and treatment. But what is true for the go-to-market strategy is also true for how J&J is concerned about the well-being of its workforce. Already in the early 20th century, the company offered its employees an on-site health center as well as a fitness center. During the 1970s, the firm started a corporate wellness program, Live for Life ®, with its aim being that its employees become some of the healthiest in the world. The impact is considerable: The company health stats are consistently better than the national averages in the U.S. One compelling example of many: while 30% of the U.S. population in 2016 suffered from hypertension, the J&J equivalent was just 9.2%. This also has a commercial impact since its healthcare costs are consistently lower compared to similarly sized organizations in the U.S. Beyond the direct health programs, J&J is leading in other areas as well: Parental leave for both moms and dads, military leave, and adoption and surrogacy assistance show the breadth of care that its employees recognize. In the 2017 Glassdoor review, 86% of J&J reviewers on the site recommended J&J as a preferred employer.

It is also very clear that the firm's strategic principles are perfectly aligned with their purpose and credo. Four key principles[21] guide the operations in a very successful manner:

----

20   https://www.jnj.com/latest-news/johnson-johnson-named-glassdoor-best-places-work-2018

21   http://www-careers-jnj-com.jnjnab25.jnj.com/sites/default/files/careers-files/pdf/JJStrategic_Framework_121206.pdf

- Broadly based in Human Health Care

- Managed for the Long Term

- Decentralized Management Approach

- Our People and Values

The values are equally straightforward and easy to understand—which is a pre-requisite to achieving support and guiding the shared behaviors of a corporation:

- growth and innovation

- investing in the future

- global diversity

- citizenship and sustainability

- developing diversity, and

- global supply base

This is a very solid framework that has been consistently updated but that has never lost its roots from the days of 1943 when the first credo was written.

Capture the Spirit

Alex Gorsky's farewell email as CEO captures the spirit of Johnson & Johnson and its corporate soul. The company established a clear ecosystem of vision, mission, and values revolved around a shared purpose. What about spirit then? *Collins Dictionary*[22] is always a good source for definitions. Let's start there by defining three key words: spirit, capture, and catching. A noun, a verb, and an adjective are the key words to understanding what this is about:

- - - - - - - - - - - -

22   https://www.collinsdictionary.com/dictionary/english/capture-the-spirit-of; https://www.collinsdictionary.com/dictionary/english/catching

- **spirit** (spɪrɪt)—singular noun: "A particular kind of spirit is the set of ideas, beliefs, and aims that are held by a group of people."

- **capture** (kæptʃəʳ)—verb: "If something or someone captures a particular quality, feeling, or atmosphere, they represent or express it successfully."

- **catching** (kætʃɪŋ)—adjective: "If a feeling or emotion is catching, it has a strong influence on other people and spreads quickly, for example through a crowd. Synonyms: infectious, contagious, transferrable, communicable."

> **Spirit is very catching in a company.**

Now, let's put all of these together: "The set of ideas, beliefs, and aims . . . held by a group . . . express it successfully . . . has a strong influence on other people and spreads quickly . . . " *Spirit is very catching in a company.*

Lexico[23] adds to the *Collins Dictionary* when it comes to the word *spirit*:

- "The prevailing or typical quality, mood, or attitude of a person, group, or period of time: 'I hope the team will build on this spirit of confidence.'"

- "The attitude or intentions with which someone undertakes or regards something."

- "The quality of courage, energy, and determination: 'His visitors admired his spirit and good temper.'"

It is those qualities of courage, energy, and determination that make spirit such an irresistible source of power for any company. It complements the other elements of shared understanding (vision, mission, values) that revolve around a shared purpose, allowing for the shared

----

23   https://www.lexico.com/definition/spirit

behaviors required to develop corporate soul. If and when that happens, something magical occurs: Spirit becomes something like a never-ending fuel to all stakeholders.

Embracing the Spirit of Your Company

Back in 2013, Michele Norsa, CEO of Salvatore Ferragamo, shared his thoughts with *The New York Times* after seven years at the helm of the family-owned luxury company. He had spent his career in family-owned companies (Rizzoli, Benetton, and Marzotto). "You must also embrace the spirit of the company," he said. "Every family is different and has different interests." He reflects on what every manager who has spent time in a family-owned business has experienced: To succeed in such an environment, it is best to learn fast what matters to the various family members. Is it their involvement in product development? Or having the final say on pricing? Or getting their voice heard on employee engagement and satisfaction? Or is it the firm's reputation that they care about most? For Michele Norsa, one lesson has been key: "For them, it's not just about profit, market share, etc.; there is another side, which is more human, more passionate."[24]

You are lucky if this spirit is in place when you start in a company. When it is not, don't try to sugarcoat the gaps by creating some nice but superficial events. Look at the whole picture. It is the *Soul System™* that enables corporations to develop a spirit that people can capture—and embrace. In the following chapters, I will guide you through the Soul System™, including its eight shared behaviors, as you work to build your company's soul. Each behavior will include "soul searching" questions to aid in your journey.

----

24   https://www.nytimes.com/2013/12/23/business/international/embracing-the-spirit-of-your-company.html

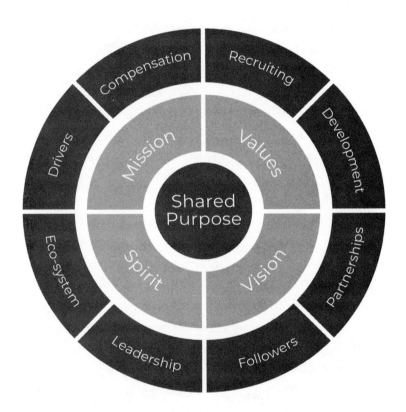

Figure 3: Shared purpose as the key to building corporate soul.

CHAPTER 3

Purpose Meets Soul

Do you have an understanding of the purpose of your company?
How is it relevant to your customers and employees—
and how would the receptionist describe it?

Chapter Goal:
- - - - - - - - - - - - -

Define your company's purpose as the foundation to building
corporate soul—and understand why *sharing that purpose* is as
important as ensuring that the content is real and that purpose
statements don't contain any advertising fluff.

We actually spend one-third of our lives at work. That's
90,000 hours over the course of a lifetime. The average
American spends over one hundred hours each year commuting on top of that—if you live your life in one of those megacities
that might be a significant underestimation—two hours a day is nothing
special. Multiplied by two hundred days a year and forty years that gets
you another 16,000 hours. Take a step back and you will probably realize

that you had better spend that time in an environment that actually has a sense of purpose beyond providing a paycheck each month.

Purpose gives us direction, motivates us, gives reason for our existence. It also helps us make decisions—big ones and small ones. *Merriam-Webster* differentiates between the various words that are synonymous with purpose: Intention, intent, design, aim, end, object, objective, and goal all mean what one intends to accomplish or attain. What makes purpose different, though, is that it "suggests a more settled determination."[25] While purpose is important for individuals, it has been recognized more and more that it is critical for business success, too.

> Purpose has become one of the "four Ps" that are becoming the global standard when corporate stakeholders are reviewing the performance of a company: people, profit, planet, and purpose.

Purpose has become one of the "four Ps" that are becoming the global standard when corporate stakeholders are reviewing the performance of a company: people, profit, planet, and purpose. While people and profit are very tangible, planet and purpose are not. Yet they are increasingly important and will come back time and again in the chapters of this book. Ernst & Young (EY) and Oxford University Saïd Business School[26] conducted a study that indicated that public conversations about purpose increased by a factor of 5 between 1995 and 2014. This study was one of the first undertakings to systematically understand and explore "the era of purpose within the context of business." But it's not just a topic in conversations; it also drives actual business performance. David Jensen, EY's global disruptive innovation and wavespace leader, said, "Predicting the future is impossible, but when an organization can articulate and activate a higher purpose it has a better opportunity to shape the future of itself and its marketplace."[27]

----

25   https://www.merriam-webster.com/dictionary/purpose

26   https://www.sbs.ox.ac.uk/news/sense-purpose

27   https://www.ey.com/en_gl/purpose/why-business-must-harness-the-power-of-purpose

Without purpose at the heart, there is no chance for soul to develop throughout the entire company. Like Harvard Business School professor Ranjay Gulati discovered in his work on start-up companies, "There's an essential, intangible something in start-ups—an energy, a soul. Company founders sense its presence. So do early employees and customers. It inspires people to contribute their talent, money, and enthusiasm and fosters a sense of deep connection and mutual purpose. As long as this spirit persists, engagement is high and start-ups remain agile and innovative, spurring growth. But when it vanishes, ventures can falter, and everyone perceives the loss—something special is gone."[28]

Do You Know Your Company's Purpose?

When founders of start-ups are trying to get funding for their great ideas, one thing that investors are looking for is not just a great business idea, but also a bigger thought that is unique. Why? Because they know that companies and brands that provide that purpose are stronger and more valuable than those that don't.

Sequoia Capital,[29] which has been in the venture capital business since 1972, has invested in over 250 companies, including Apple, Google, Oracle, PayPal, LinkedIn, Instagram, Yahoo!, and WhatsApp. The combined 2020 public market capitalization for these companies was over $1.4 trillion, equivalent to 22 percent of Nasdaq. The pitch deck structure that Sequoia recommends start-up companies use when they come to acquire investors starts with the company purpose—it's the title of the first slide.

When you look at successful start-ups like Airbnb and review their pitch decks, it becomes very clear how important purpose is to them. Here is Airbnb's pitch solution:[30] "Build a web platform where users can rent

---

28   https://hbr.org/2019/07/the-soul-of-a-start-up
29   https://en.wikipedia.org/wiki/Sequoia_Capital
30   https://de.slideshare.net/PitchDeckCoach/airbnb-first-pitch-deck-editable

out their space to host travelers to (a) save money when traveling, (b) make money when hosting and (c) share culture through a local connection to the city." Airbnb successfully turned that solution statement into the foundation of the company itself, and this has allowed Airbnb to build a culture and create a corporate soul that is unique to it. Now it has come quite a ways from those early days to the well-crafted expression of its purpose of today: "Airbnb and its community want to create a world where Anyone can Belong Anywhere."[31] Douglas John Atkin, Airbnb's global head of community from 2012 to 2017, defined the quality of a purpose statement very clearly: "So, a purpose should be grounded in an everyday reality, but be able to stretch to an improbable goal. Ideally, one that wants to make the world a better place."

Clarity and simplicity are key features of any purpose statement. Without that clarity, it will be impossible for it to make its way through the organization and create real relevance for its current and future customers. But when that clarity is found, the real job starts. You need that level of simplicity when you want to ensure that virtually everybody in your company understands its reason for being. The impact is massive—is it understood through the ranks or is it just a boardroom PowerPoint exercise?

Does it give meaning to the receptionist, as well as the salesperson or the engineer? In Airbnb's case, is it understood by the hosts that their guests come to them as those "anyone" individuals who "can belong anywhere"? This galvanizing thought that captures why the company exists in the first place fuels the soul that this company obviously has.

Purpose becomes the foundation of your business's strategy and the basis to create the value proposition for all stakeholders. Robert S. Kaplan, professor for accounting from Harvard Business School, and David P. Norton, president of Renaissance Solutions Inc., are very clear about it.[32]

----

31   https://medium.com/@douglas.atkin/how-airbnb-found-its-purpose-and-why-its-a-good-one-b5c987c0c216

32   Robert S. Kaplan, and David P. Norton. *Strategy Maps: Converting Intangible Assets into Tangible Outcomes*. Boston: Harvard Business School Press, 2004.

"Strategy is based on a differentiated customer value proposition. Satisfying customers is the source of sustainable value creation." In 2000 they stated that the customer value proposition describes "the unique mix of product and service attributes, customer relations, and corporate image that a company offers." It actually is a promise of value to be delivered, communicated, and acknowledged. It is also a belief and an expectation from the customer about how value (benefit) will be delivered, experienced, and acquired. A value proposition can apply to an entire organization, or parts thereof, or customer accounts, or products or services. While differentiation from competition is key to a company developing and establishing relationships with its potential customers, Kaplan and Norton emphasize that the value proposition is critical for linking the internal organization to improved customer outcomes.

These customer outcomes have become increasingly influenced by the reputation of companies. The 2018 Edelman Trust Barometer[33] states that 63 percent of all respondents agree with this statement: "A good reputation may get me to try a product—but unless I come to trust the company behind the product, I will soon stop buying it, regardless of its reputation." The same study across 28 markets globally confirms that 52 percent of the general population trusts businesses versus a 43 percent trust level toward governments. While it shines a dark light on the trust level between citizens and their government, the light on corporations is brighter—even though pretty much half (48 percent) of all members of the general population also do not trust businesses. Regarding the role of the CEO, the Edelman Trust Barometer notes that 77 percent expect the CEO to be personally visible in each business situation, and 84 percent expect the head of the firm to inform conversations and policy debates on one or more issues. Seventy-four percent agree CEOs should be personally visible in discussing work their company has done

--- --- --- --- ---

33   https://www.edelman.com/sites/g/files/aatuss191/files/2018-10/Edelman_Trust_
      Barometer_Implications_for_CEOs_2018.pdf

to benefit society. High expectations—an overwhelming 79 percent agree that CEOs should be personally visible in sharing the company's purpose and vision. In other words, delivering a shared purpose, creating a shared understanding, and ensuring shared behaviors. (The question "Which is more believable about a company: CEOs or employees?" came in at 71 percent to 29 percent in favor of the employees.) If the purpose isn't shared, the understanding isn't shared and the behaviors aren't shared, so guess whose reputation employees will share?

Walk the Talk

The differentiated value proposition is key to winning consumers who buy products and services from brands. But it is not enough alone; it has to be in sync with the corporate value proposition. When these aren't in sync, customers will vote with their feet and their purses. When customers smell the flavor of corporations not walking the talk that they promise in shiny and glossy ads, they react immediately, which impacts businesses immediately. The more noble an organization's purpose, the tougher the consequences. The EY study on harnessing the power of purpose highlights the communication challenges that go along with corporate behavior. "Diminishing brand control, rising social media" is the headline under which EY concludes that "in recent years businesses have lost some control over their brands to customers and the wider public. The public has proven adept at harnessing social media to propagate their influence and opinions on unfulfilled brand promises around the world in seconds—faster and more effectively than any news organization could. The ease with which opinions can be expressed makes creating a positive first impression more important than ever."[34]

Let's look at Oxfam. This is a huge conglomeration of nongovernmental organizations with thousands of employees in over ninety

---

34   https://www.ey.com/en_gl/purpose/why-business-must-harness-the-power-of-purpose

countries in the world. Oxfam recognizes the universality and indivisibility of human rights, and in November 2000, it adopted a rights-based approach as the framework for all the work of the confederation and its partners. It developed these overarching aims to express these rights in practical terms:[35]

- The right to a sustainable livelihood
- The right to basic social services
- The right to life and security
- The right to be heard
- The right to an identity

Today, Oxfam's six goals focus on putting local communities and the voices of poor people at the center of change—its best hope for ending the injustice of poverty. The organization claims its work "is always rooted in a vision of a world where women and men are valued and treated equally, able to influence the decisions that affect their lives and meet their responsibilities as full citizens."[36]

The six new goals are as follows:

1. Help people claim their right to a better life
2. Champion equal rights for women
3. Save lives, now and in the future
4. Safeguard global food supplies
5. Help people claim a fairer share of natural resources
6. Increase money for basic services

- - - - - - - - - - - -

35   *Oxfam International Strategic Plan 2007–2012: Demanding Justice.* Oxfam International.

36   https://www.oxfam.org.uk/what-we-do/about-us/how-we-work/our-goals-and-values

What happened between the two sets of goals? In 2017 UK newspaper *The Times* reported that in 2011, a senior member of the Oxfam team had been discovered paying for prostitutes in Haiti—the year after Hurricane Tomas had hit the island. Rather than firing the individual, his manager decided to make him resign—not quite what you would expect after the investigation confirmed the deed. When this was announced to the press, a social media flame war was the consequence. It hit the news way beyond Haiti. It was really no surprise that the integrity and reputation of the entire organization suffered. Donors started to leave, funders stepped back, ambassadors quit.

The integrity of the entire organization and all of its work was called into question. Oxfam's reputation had been irreparably damaged. Oxfam had been forced to make 16 million GBP[37] in cuts to its staff and programs. That flame war based on an organizational governance failure had long-lasting consequences. Lesson learned: Nonprofit organizations need to deal with their organizational behavior very carefully as the moral compass that guides them is viewed much more critically than for-profit companies. If you claim to do good, you cannot accept any failures in behavior anywhere from anyone.

Crisis Demands Leaders to Search for the Soul of the Company

Sometimes companies lose their focus, or they do not understand the shifts in technologies or societal behavior that have a lasting impact on their offering. The great ones see it before it hits them. Of those that don't see it coming, only a few actually remind themselves of their purpose.

LEGO is a perfect example of a company that lost its way but then found its raison d'être again. The company's purpose is to inspire and develop children to think creatively, reason systematically, and release their potential to

---

37   https://www.tbd.community/en/a/road-hell-paved-shitstorms

shape their own future—experiencing the endless human possibility. This purpose connects very clearly with its vision statement: "Inventing the future of play. We want to pioneer new ways of playing, play materials and the business models of play—leveraging globalization and digitalization . . . it is not just about products, it is about realizing the human possibility."[38] And their mission is to "inspire and develop the builders of tomorrow."

When Jørgen Vig Knudstorp took over the leadership at LEGO back in 2003, he had to start a fight for survival. The company had diversified into theme parks, design studios, and many new different lines of product. This focus on product launches kept LEGO growing but killed the bottom line. More importantly, though, all these new lines of product did not convey what had been "LEGO-ness" ever since the company had become the maker of children's favorite toy. If you think about it in the way professor and philosopher Charles Handy did, you will get to one very simple conclusion: The company had lost its soul.

Consumers had noticed and voted with their purchase decisions. The significant drop in sales put LEGO against the ropes.

It was a tough situation, but as the old adage goes, "Crisis is both danger and opportunity." It has the power to become a turning point. But you have to accept it and not neglect it. That's what Knudstorp did. In an interview with Egon Zehnder Consultancy, he explained how he turned the company around.

> Egon Zehnder Consultancy: When you assumed the position of CEO in very difficult times, you said that the LEGO Group had lost its soul. What exactly had been lost and how would you describe the soul of the company today?
>
> Jørgen Vig Knudstorp: So, while we need to make money, the LEGO Group has a deeper purpose than that. Our

---

38   https://www.academia.edu/40161778/Mission_Inspire_and_develop_the_builders_
     of_tomorrow

purpose is to make a difference in children's lives by giving them wonderful play experiences, and bringing this experience to every child on the planet. Money is like oxygen to a body, but none of us sit in this room to breathe the air; we sit in this room to fulfill a purpose with our lives. Making money is the entry ticket to fulfilling that purpose. In the past we had "religious" people, if you like, who believed in the purpose of what we did, but we also had "realists" who saw this purely as a business. I wanted to combine the two in individuals—people who could succeed in the marketplace and also reflect the spirit, purpose and energy of the company. This goes to the soul of our company.[39]

Knudstorp is one of the few business leaders who uses the word *soul* as they talk about the culture of their companies. His statement refers to it as the sum of spirit, purpose, and energy. These are the ingredients that need to be aligned, as this is what it takes to ensure a company can reach its full potential. LEGO had lost its purpose and all the elements of its shared understanding about its roots. Without those roots, how can anyone create shared behavior activities in a way that stays true to the company? So, it was not a surprise that Knudstorp arrived at his statement about spirit, purpose, and energy.

LEGO's experience proves the point that Jim Stengel makes in his book *Grow*: A business never leaves its heritage behind, any more than a living organism leaves its original DNA behind. And like DNA, the heritage isn't static and unchanging. A business's leaders, employees, and customers—along with its outside environment—constantly influence its ongoing heritage. Stengel quotes Joey Reiman, CEO of BrightHouse consulting: "When I hear about a company moving backwards, I get

- - - - - - - - - - - -

39   https://www.egonzehnder.com/video/the-Lego-group-ceo-Jorgen-vig-knudstorp-is-building-more-than-a-toy-company

excited."[40] That's where it starts—for companies that have been around, it is about why they have permission to exist today; for start-ups, it is why there is a need for their product or service that has not been satisfied before.

LEGO's return was widely recognized. One of the most compelling pieces of research that shows the impact of its renaissance is the annual study from The Reputation Institute (RepTrak Company™).[41] It runs the Global CSR RepTrak list—and LEGO is probably *the* success story of the 2011–2020 decade.

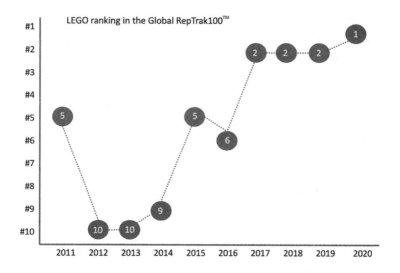

Figure 4: Global RepTrak100 ranking of LEGO 2011–2020.

There is obviously not just one secret recipe behind that impressive graph. But before we look into the key reasons why and how LEGO delivered those impressive results, there are more insights when looking into the

- - - - - - - - - - - -

40   Jim Stengel. *Grow: How Ideals Power Growth and Profit at the World's Greatest Companies*. New York: Crown Business, 2011.

41   https://www.reptrak.com

top ten companies and their ranking in the Global RepTrak100: LEGO and Walt Disney Company are the only companies that have appeared in the top ten *every* year. One company ranked in the top position four times: Rolex (2016, 2017, 2018, and 2019); the watchmaker has been in the top ten since 2013. BMW made it to the top three times (2012, 2013, and 2015) with eight appearances in the top ten. Tech giants Google and Apple did not make it in 2019 and 2020, whereas Microsoft and Intel made it to the top ten in both those years. The rise of entertainment brand Netflix landed it at seventh in 2019 and 2020, as well as newcomers Ferrari (fourth) and Levi's (sixth) in both years.

What is it that LEGO is getting right here? RepTrak suggests the success is based on three pillars:

1. Excellent products and services

2. Leading with innovation

3. Growing with purpose

Its 2020 report, *A Decade of Reputation Leaders*, explains it this way:

> LEGO and Walt Disney achieved very strong perceptions for their products and services over the last decade. There is widespread, international buy-in around the quality of what these companies offer in the market—both get strong to excellent scores in "high quality products and services" across all 15 markets. This is the number one most important business attribute in terms of reputation impact. After products and services, both companies received credit for their leadership and sustained innovation. They have adapted and expanded their core product offerings to the shift in consumer expectations. LEGO is a top-of-mind brand in terms of children's products, while simultaneously improving the sustainability of its products and offering ways to play in real life and

virtual reality. Both LEGO and Walt Disney perform according to consumer expectations while also being intentional about their corporate purpose and the social impact of their business. In fact, *both companies are among the top 15 global companies when it comes to purpose.*

The Impact of Purpose

Swiss publisher Hans Ringier is a great example of a leader who embodied the soul of their company. When he turned eighty years old—he had already handed the publishing house leadership over to his sons Christoph and Michael—the internal corporate magazine celebrated him as "the soul of the company."[42] The article describes the power of corporate soul: "Does a company need to have a soul? Isn't it enough when managers sort things as they would do in any other company? It is not enough. It takes soul! And soul only rarely remains on its own. Where leadership appreciates people, people are going. One rather buys into people than companies." This approach was part and parcel of the success he had in making the publishing house Switzerland's largest in the eighties and nineties.

> Embodying the corporate soul is only possible when the values of the company and the values of the individual are aligned.

Ringier's impact was significant—even though he did not found the company. Why? Because he was able to win hearts and convince minds, and because he embodied the corporate soul of the enterprise his father had founded decades ago that allowed the corporation to be a key player in the industry even in the modern age.

Embodying the corporate soul is only possible when the values of the company and the values of the individual are aligned. In the best sense of

----

42   Jan-Otmar Hesse. "Seele des Unternehmens." *Das stille Unternehmertum Hans Ringiers.* 2014.

the word, it is a value proposition come to life. But this alignment is not sufficient. EY identifies[43] six forces that are at play:

- The trust deficit
- Sustainability
- Social inequality
- Diminishing brand control and rising social media
- Demand for longer-term thinking
- Digitization—threats and opportunities

EY's "harnessing the power of purpose" study concludes that "grasping the core reason [for] an organization's existence and seeing how that sits within the wider world can be a more constructive way to address disruption." I couldn't agree more in a world where all stakeholders—be it communities and customers, investors and employees—are asking every business about the role it wants to play in society. "The need for purpose may be driven by global socio-economic factors seemingly beyond the control of corporations. But there is an upside: much of the discussion about purpose suggests that companies perform better if they have a clear sense of purpose. Purpose-driven companies make more money; have more engaged employees and more loyal customers; and are even better at innovation and transformational change." This EY summary sends a powerful message to leaders across all businesses.

> "Purpose-driven companies make more money; have more engaged employees and more loyal customers; and are even better at innovation and transformational change."

- - - - - - - - - - -

43   https://www.ey.com/es_ar/purpose/why-business-must-harness-the-power-of-purpose

Three-quarters of executives at purposeful companies reported that the integration of purpose creates value in the short-term, as well as over the long run for their companies, according to EY's findings.

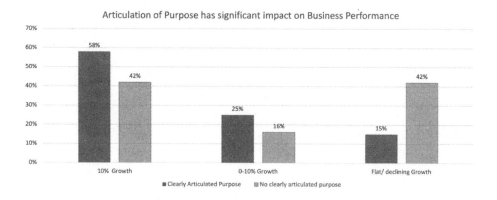

Articulation of Purpose has significant impact on Business Performance

Figure 5: Articulation of Purpose—EY 2018: Why business needs to harness the power of purpose.

"The sense of being part of something greater than yourself can lead to high levels of engagement, high levels of creativity and the willingness to partner across functional and product boundaries within a company, which are hugely powerful," said Rebecca Henderson,[44] the John and Natty McArthur University Professor at Harvard Business School. "Once they're past a certain financial threshold, many people are as motivated by intrinsic meaning and the sense that they are contributing to something worthwhile as much as they are by financial returns or status."

The Harvard Business Review–EY study "The Business Case for Purpose" confirms the impact purpose has on business success. Purpose is the stamp in the passport that has the power to drive an enterprise forward faster. But it is not only about speed—the quality of transformation

- - - - - - - - - - - -

44   https://www.ey.com/Publication/vwLUAssets/ey-the-business-case-for-purpose/$FILE/ey-the-business-case-for-purpose.pdf

and future innovation increases when purpose becomes a shared purpose: "53 percent of executives who said their company has a strong sense of purpose (prioritizers) said their organization is successful with innovation and transformation efforts, compared with 31 percent of those trying to articulate a sense of purpose (developers) and 19 percent of the companies who have not thought about it at all (laggards)."[45]

When you think about it, it makes all the sense in the world. Remember the point from the beginning of this chapter: What is true for individuals is also true for corporations. If a company is convinced to do the right thing, its people will do it with so much more passion and conviction, and it will show. You will be on your way to success—who is going to stop you?

Purpose That Really Matters

It goes without saying that purpose on its own will not get you or your company there. If you have not done your homework when it comes to your offering of products or services, the market you are operating in, and the target customers, "purpose only" is not the answer. But purpose that matters to your target customers can ignite your performance and growth significantly. "The Business Case for Purpose" study indicates that 88 percent of executives believe that a clearly articulated purpose is creating value for the customer. Global consumers reinforce that notion, as 72 percent would recommend a company that has a purpose.

An analysis[46] by LinkedIn and Imperative confirms that thinking—85 percent of purpose-led companies show positive business growth versus 42 percent of non-purpose-led companies that experienced a drop in growth.

----

45   https://www.ey.com/en_uk/purpose/why-business-must-harness-the-power-of-purpose

46   https://business.linkedin.com/content/dam/me/business/en-us/talent-solutions/resources/pdfs/purpose-at-work-global-report.pdf

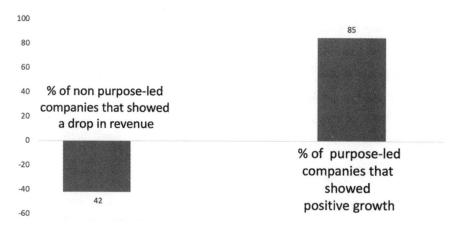

Figure 6: 2016 global report on purpose at work by LinkedIn and Imperative.

But not everything that is labeled *purpose* stands the test. Tom Roach, who has worked as a strategist in various advertising agencies, published on his blog a critical view on the inflation of purpose as the holy grail.[47] He focuses on brand purpose rather than corporate purpose and distinguishes between three different types of brands:

- Brands that he says are Born Purposeful—"often founder-led, small, niche, and usually founded with a societal purpose and where purpose goes across the whole business operation."

- Brands that he calls Corporate Converts—"often larger businesses that have adopted the concept of purpose more recently."

- Brands that he labels Pseudo-purposeful—"ones for which purpose is just a new ad campaign claiming to try and solve an issue

- - - - - - - - - - -

47   https://thetomroach.com/2020/06/23/truth-lies-and-brand-purpose-the-biggest-lie-the-ad-industry-ever-told/

like gender or racial equality, or toxic masculinity or whatever the most resonant topic is that their social listening data says is trending with their demographic that month."

Roach's conclusion is pretty sound: "The likelihood of purpose driving a profit probably decreases from type 1 to 3." I could not agree more. If purpose becomes the task marketing and advertising have to *create*, then you will never get the authenticity that Jørgen Vig Knudstorp reestablished at LEGO or that Jeff Weiner established at LinkedIn.

Procter & Gamble (P&G) also has been able to walk that fine line between authenticity and purpose. The company prides itself on its "Honest Business Ethics," with roots that go back to 1887.[48] Staying true to those principles and pushing to make them relevant in today's world is what P&G is striving to do. It is identifying a relevant meaning to all stakeholders—both internal and external—and is aligning its activities and actions against that meaning. P&G's push to become "a force for good and a force for growth" is the basis for sharing content that is connected to its purpose and valued by its customers at the same time. As long as the company's actions and behaviors are true to that purpose, this approach works. It is a sound approach aligned with the business. But it makes it even more important to ensure that those behaviors and actions remain sound.

"I think that the 5 billion people in the world who we serve are looking around and saying, 'we need to make sure that we leave this world in a better place' and that has to come from the everyday household and personal care products that we use as well. So, we made a very deliberate decision to build things like sustainability and equality and inclusion into the business to make it part of how brands grow and part of the business model," says Marc Pritchard, P&G's chief brand officer.[49]

----

48   https://us.pg.com/pg-history/

49   https://www.forbes.com/sites/afdhelaziz/2019/07/16/the-power-of-purpose-how-procter-and-gamble-is-becoming-a-force-for-good-a-force-for-growth-pt1/

The company's work on diversity has focused on elevating women into senior positions; the percentage of positions filled by women moved up from 5 percent in 1992 to over 30 percent in 2011. P&G claims "Diversity in Everything We Do,"[50] and it even trademarked its program "Everyone valued. Everyone included. Everyone performing at their peak™." Pritchard shared his perspective in an interview with Afdhel Aziz, the founder and chief purpose officer of Conspiracy of Love, a brand purpose consultancy. Pritchard refers to a personal experience many years ago when he and his family spent time at a spiritual retreat: "And at the end of it, the guy who led it said, 'I hope you know the good you can do because you're in business—and business will someday be the greatest force for good in the future. It won't be the powers that be today, it'll be business.'"[51]

An example of the dynamics that unfold when you apply that logic is the CoverGirl brand. Pritchard brought a more diverse and inclusive approach to beauty to the brand—and as a result began to understand in reality the potential of using advertising activities to actually change the cultural conversation. More recent examples of racial and gender equality campaigns include the famous "The Talk" commercial in 2017 and later on with "The Look" ad—a story about bias in America—in 2019. Only a year later, America faced significant unrest when George Floyd, a forty-six-year-old Black man, was killed in Minneapolis by a white policeman. Over 2,000 cities in the United States and countries all over the world saw protest gatherings happening in support of the Black Lives Matter movement.

In moments like these, brands have a voice, but consumers have a very fine sense of what is just driven by commercial goals and what is driven by genuine—or authentic—business ethics. For P&G, it is the latter. "P&G Threatens to Pull Ad Spend If Platforms Don't Take 'Systemic Action' over Racial Equality"[52] was the *Marketing Week* headline just a month after Floyd's

- - - - - - - - - - -

50   https://us.pg.com/pg-history/

51   https://www.forbes.com/sites/afdhelaziz/2019/07/16/the-power-of-purpose-how-procter-and-gamble-is-becoming-a-force-for-good-a-force-for-growth-pt1/

52   https://www.marketingweek.com/procter-gamble-pull-spend-black-lives-matter/

death. Pritchard was quoted: "People want tangible evidence of what brands and companies stand for, and what they are doing. All brands should take the time to learn the history of the US and how it has impacted Black American communities." He conceded that P&G has a long road ahead to achieve its goals. But he said the company will accelerate changes that will make a practical difference. These will include a push to improve and increase representation of people of color throughout the creative supply chain, including brands, agencies, and production crews. Starting in the United States, P&G aspires to reach 40 percent multicultural representation within the company.

Different Owners—Still the Same Purpose Throughout

One of the prime examples of a company that has maintained a consistent purpose is Volvo. The Swedish automotive company centered its purpose on safety as defined by its founders. They stated in the very early days that "Cars are driven by people. Therefore the guiding principle behind everything we make at Volvo is—and must remain—safety."[53] Even with sales declining during the 2008 global financial crisis and the subsequent sale of the company from Ford, Volvo stayed true to its purpose, and its reinvigorated sales bear that out.

Volvo's brand video takes great pride in referencing that "this emphasis on safety, people, and quality has been a feature of our cars ever since. An innate Swedish focus on social well-being has defined the Volvo brand and been the soul of our philosophy ever since."[54] As every company and brand faces ups and downs in its history, Volvo has been no exception. But its renewed focus on what drove its initial success made it probably one of the most admired turnaround cases in the automotive industry.

On March 28, 2010, Zhejiang Geely Holding (Geely) acquired Volvo from the Ford Motor Company in the midst of the global financial

- - - - - - - - - - -

53   https://www.media.volvocars.com/global/en-gb/media/pressreleases/11381

54   https://www.youtube.com/watch?v=1Ja9gzsh8So

crisis. Ford sold its entire premier automotive group portfolio of brands. Geely's acquisition clearly stands out. A decade later, with many critical decisions, including developing a portfolio that allowed the brand to become a fully fledged alternative in the premium segment, Volvo has delivered six consecutive sales records and record profits. In 2019 the company handed more than 700,000 cars over to customers worldwide, a new record number. The Brand Finance Global 500 Index[55] shows Volvo ranking at 106 (a climb from 123), making the brand the most valuable non-German premium automotive brand. Ironically, the Ford Motor Company ranks only at 94, two positions down from the previous year.

As the Volvo brand developed into premium segments, it stayed true to its positioning on safety. During the COVID-19 pandemic, it took the promise of safety to a new level. When people were afraid to visit shops and showrooms, Volvo offered a "Stay Home Store" in seven European countries, allowing customers to buy their car with maximum social distancing in place—online with home delivery—giving "safety" a new meaning beyond the road.

Safety has been the red thread of Volvo since its early days with several remarkable milestones along the way. Volvo engineer Nils Bohlin designed the revolutionary three-point safety belt back in the late 1950s, which the brand claims has probably saved more than one million lives.[56] The company waived its patent rights, allowing every manufacturer to put these seatbelts into their cars as well. In the midst of the baby boomer decade, Volvo also took care of in-car child safety by testing the world's first rear-facing child seat, and only a decade later it launched the world's first child booster cushion. In 1976, the US government identified Volvo's 240 model as the benchmark in advanced safety to set the safety standards for all new cars.

- - - - - - - - - - - -

55 https://brandirectory.com/download-report/brand-finance-global-500-2020-preview.pdf

56 https://www.volvocars.com/mm/why-volvo/human-innovation/future-of-driving/safety/a-million-more

Volvo's mission had been to make people's lives safer and less complicated: "At Volvo Cars, everything we do starts with people. So our mission to make people's lives easier, safer and better is something that comes naturally to us. It's the Volvo way."[57] And the company publicly claims the actions that stem from this mission statement. One of its goals from 2016 is directly linked: "By 2020 no one should be killed or seriously injured in a new Volvo."[58] New technologies that are making cars smarter are at play—and many of these technologies are being made available to other car companies. But Volvo has probably developed the biggest synchronicity between its heart and soul and the innovations it is putting into its products.

In 2020, Volvo's mission statement evolved to "driving prosperity through transport and infrastructure solutions," connecting it with a bold vision "to be the most desired and successful transport and infrastructure solution provider in the world."[59]

Under Geely's ownership, Volvo embarked on a growth pattern, but the clarity of purpose that had been the soul of the Volvo brand since its founders Assar Gabrielsson and Gustaf Larson started the journey in 1924 remained just as strong during the second decade of the twenty-first century.

Whether it is geographical expansion; leadership changes; product or service portfolio revisions; activities in the merger and acquisitions space; or engaging in major transformational activities; all of these complex decisions are much easier to make when you have a clear and honest understanding of your purpose.

It is that understanding of purpose that allows companies to take the next step: building the corporate soul through shared understanding and shared behaviors.

- - - - - - - - - - - -

57   https://www.volvocars.com/uk/about/our-company/this-is-volvo-cars

58   https://www.fastcompany.com/3056754/volvo-launches-vision-2020-aiming-for-zero-car-related-deaths

59   https://www.volvogroup.com/en/about-us/our-mission-vison-and-aspirations.html

Key thoughts to consider on
defining your company's purpose

	Soul Searching in Action
✓	Do you have an understanding of the purpose of your company?
✓	Does your management team share that sense of purpose?
✓	Is this purpose grounded in an everyday reality and at the same time able to stretch to an improbable goal?
✓	Does it even want to make the world a better place?
✓	Or is it just a pseudo-purpose—an advertising trick?
✓	How is it relevant to your customers and employees?
✓	How would the receptionist describe it to a visitor—is it a truly shared purpose?
✓	Are you personally prepared to act upon that purpose statement?

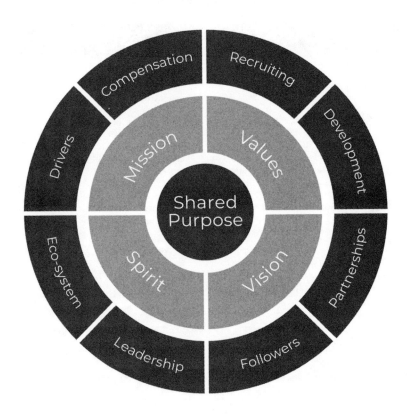

Figure 7: Complete elements of the Soul System™.

CHAPTER 4

Understand the Soul of Your Company

What is it that makes your company unique in the way it deals with employees, with customers, with suppliers, and with other stakeholders—what manifests the soul of your company?

Chapter Goal:

Define your company's culture in one sentence and make the company's soul recognizable for all stakeholders.

The Soul System™ can get into full swing when all elements of shared understanding—mission, vision, values, spirit—and the corresponding shared behaviors are completely internalized by everyone in a company. A company's culture is a manifestation of its corporate soul. The shared behaviors that drive that culture are either true to the soul of the firm—or not. In both cases, understanding your company's soul is key. Why is that important and what makes it so difficult?

Successful start-ups develop their culture beyond the leadership spirit very naturally, as they are often driven by the sheer motivation to do things differently. Airbnb's CEO Brian Chesky is famous for his quote, "Culture is simply a shared way of doing something with passion."[60] But as simple as it sounds, it is one of the most difficult things to achieve when a company grows beyond the founding partners.

> A company's culture is a manifestation of its corporate soul. The shared behaviors that drive that culture are either true to the soul of the firm—or not.

By having a strong sense of your company's corporate soul—and if everyone inside the firm is a role model for its shared purpose—the company has a far better chance to withstand that growth beyond the start-up stage and the various trials and downturns along the way.

The COVID-19 pandemic, for instance, has been a significant headwind for many companies. Especially in the hospitality category, the damage has been immense. Airbnb is a good example. Chesky had to manage a situation that many leaders were confronted with: reducing the company's workforce significantly. In Airbnb's case this meant letting 1,900 out of 7,500 employees go—25 percent of the entire staff. Chesky embodies the soul of Airbnb, so his response to the COVID-19 crisis reflected that soul in a very personal way. He sent an email to all staff on May 5, 2020, outlining the difficult decision to reduce the staff but also providing clear and transparent language on what steps the company was taking to help those who were losing their jobs. In addressing his colleagues, who all bought into the purpose of this category-changing company, Chesky found words of humility and compassion, of humanity and selflessness, and, even more importantly, of honor. The following is an excerpt from Chesky's email—it will most likely be found in leadership books for decades to come. You can read the entire email in the appendix:[61]

----

60   https://www.brainyquote.com/quotes/brian_chesky _919289

61   https://news.airbnb.com/a-message-from-co-founder-and-ceo-brian-chesky/

Today, I must confirm that we are reducing the size of the Airbnb workforce. For a company like us whose mission is centered around belonging, this is incredibly difficult to confront, and it will be even harder for those who have to leave Airbnb. I am going to share as many details as I can on how I arrived at this decision, what we are doing for those leaving, and what will happen next . . .

How we approached reductions

It was important that we had a clear set of principles, guided by our core values, for how we would approach reductions in our workforce. These were our guiding principles:

- Map all reductions to our future business strategy and the capabilities we will need.

- Do as much as we can for those who are impacted.

- Be unwavering in our commitment to diversity.

- Optimize for 1:1 communication for those impacted.

- Wait to communicate any decisions until all details are landed—transparency of only partial information can make matters worse . . .

The result is that we will have to part with teammates that we love and value. We have great people leaving Airbnb, and other companies will be lucky to have them. To take care of those that are leaving, we have looked across severance, equity, healthcare, and job support and done our best to treat everyone in a compassionate and thoughtful way.

As I have learned these past eight weeks, a crisis brings you clarity about what is truly important. Though we have been through a whirlwind, some things are more clear to me than ever before.

First, I am thankful for everyone here at Airbnb. Throughout this harrowing experience, I have been inspired by all of you. Even in the worst of circumstances, I've seen the very best of us. The world needs human connection now more than ever, and I know that Airbnb will rise to the occasion. I believe this because I believe in you.

Second, I have a deep feeling of love for all of you. Our mission is not merely about travel. When we started Airbnb, our original tagline was, "Travel like a human." The human part was always more important than the travel part. What we are about is belonging, and at the center of belonging is love.

To those of you staying, one of the most important ways we can honor those who are leaving is for them to know that their contributions mattered, and that they will always be part of Airbnb's story. I am confident their work will live on, just like this mission will live on.

To those leaving Airbnb, I am truly sorry. Please know this is not your fault. The world will never stop seeking the qualities and talents that you brought to Airbnb . . . that helped make Airbnb. I want to thank you, from the bottom of my heart, for sharing them with us.

Brian

While Chesky's message was a tough one, it conveyed a spirit of empathy that recognized the value that every recipient brought to the company, whether they were leaving or staying. It is often said in times of redundancies that "this is nothing personal." It is always personal. But Chesky's message shows how to explain a situation in a very personal way, thereby making it less of a personal feat for the recipient. Remember the subtitle of this chapter: What is it that makes your company unique in the way it deals with employees? This email represents the uniqueness of Airbnb probably at its best: the sense of belonging—even when 1,900 individuals will no longer belong as employees to the corporation.

This sense of belonging is critical to Airbnb's soul, and this notion became the undercurrent of the entire email. Yes, 1,900 individuals were not going to belong to Airbnb as employees anymore, but as Chesky stated, "What we are about is belonging, and at the center of belonging is love. . . . *One of the most important ways we can honor those who are leaving is for them to know that their contributions mattered, and that they will always be part of Airbnb's story.*" With these words he offered the opportunity that they will continue to belong in spirit. The empathy—the soul—that comes through helped to ensure that this massive exit did not become a blame game. He did not question their professional skills, which is really critical when you consider that all of these people needed to be motivated to find their next destination. The last thing they needed in this situation was to lose faith in their abilities.

In fact, Chesky gave them hope by saying "other companies will be lucky to have them." He was so sure that they had been hiring the right people all along the way, and so any future employer would benefit from the fact that these people had been Airbnb people. Plus, the creation of a public-facing website to find employment for these teammates, as he called them, was a significant point of support, as well as dedicating a "significant portion of Airbnb recruiting" to the placement of alumni. The way Chesky honors those who are leaving is second to none. Very often exits have a sense of public executions. This one was the total opposite. No obligations like "hand over your phone, your laptop, leave the building, no conversations with current employees." In fact, Chesky gave time for the conversations that are required to ensure that there was no additional threat to the individuals' mental health: "I want to give everyone the next few days to process this."

This is a classic example of how a shared purpose at the heart of the company with a corresponding shared understanding delivered through shared behaviors can hold steady even in times of severe trouble. Chesky stayed authentic to himself and true to the corporate soul of Airbnb—he really was able to avoid "breaking" the culture.

If you break the culture, you break the machine that creates your products. In 2012, one of the most reputed investors in the Silicon Valley, Peter Thiel, pointed at the importance of the unique spirit that he experienced at Airbnb when he confirmed his $150 million investment in the start-up: "Don't fuck up the culture!"[62]

A Triple Whammy: Commercial Losses, Brexit, and COVID-19

Like California-based Airbnb, Bentley Motors, based in Crewe, England, was tested by COVID-19, but the renowned luxury car brand also faced other significant challenges, both internal and external. When Adrian Hallmark arrived in 2018 as CEO and chairman, his mission was straightforward: return the company to profitability. But a looming Brexit made that goal an even bigger challenge compared to any restructuring that needed to happen. And then, of course, out of nowhere the pandemic hit the world.

A hard Brexit with no deal with the European Union or varying degrees of potential agreements? From day one when Hallmark took office, this question was all over the business. Any decision would significantly impact the commercial future of the company just one year before it would celebrate its one hundredth birthday. Given that 85 percent of the company's sales were outside the United Kingdom, the impact of Brexit was immense. In addition, the supply side was just as challenging: Forty-five percent of all components were bought-in (versus made in Crewe), and 90 percent of those bought-in components came from the EU on a just-in-time basis. Ensuring the arrival of parts from outside the United Kingdom to secure production was a key issue. That uncertainty came on top of a planned restructuring during which more than 1,200 individuals—roughly 25 percent of the overall workforce—were destined to leave the company. A perfect recipe for internal turmoil and a management team that employees would put no trust in. As if that were not enough, in March 2020 COVID-19 hit the company. Every leader who is afraid of

----

62   https://medium.com/@bchesky/dont-fuck-up-the-culture-597cde9ee9d4

managing challenges like this can learn from how Hallmark and his team approached the three challenges of Brexit, restructuring, and COVID-19 with dedication and determination. Here are ten key lessons from how Hallmark faced these challenges at Bentley that you can apply at your company. Making these lessons part of your company's shared understanding and shared behaviors will help you to strengthen the corporate soul and prepare your firm for times of crisis.[63]

Create an environment of clarity with all stakeholders.

Hallmark had to balance his efforts with the workforce in Crewe, as well as with shareholders and key stakeholders like management and unions at Volkswagen Group based in Wolfsburg, Germany. He worked to create a shared understanding about the company's purpose, vision, and mission. Having the full support of all stakeholders allowed him to implement a strategy (read more in chapter 6) that was already showing the first successes even in the most difficult year for any business—2020.

Building trust creates trust in return.

"We brought all 4,500 people together every quarter and shared openly what the issues were," Hallmark recalled. "I said, 'We have a problem; it is not your fault. But we need to solve it together.' We told them what we were going to do about it, showed them the plan, and quickly they took over and delivered faster and deeper than we expected." The information that was shared at these meetings was not the usual summary slides that would hide the difficult details. The management team shared everything that those in the boardroom were privy to with everybody inside the

----

63   Adrian Hallmark, in an interview with the author.

company. In companies that lack corporate soul, you would see details like that leaked to the media soon after. Not here: The trust that Hallmark and his management team offered was paid back big time. No confidential details left the company walls—a major sign of a fully intact corporate soul. These all-hands meetings were accompanied by sessions with smaller groups of people, where issues were discussed in depth. Pulse surveys, a regular barometer of employee feeling, showed that this level of mutual trust created much more openness when it came to admitting—and thereby identifying—issues. In 2018, only 20 percent of employees answered the question "Do you feel safe in admitting problems?" in the affirmative. In 2020, that number had grown to 80 percent.

Treat your people as human beings.

"We managed the unavoidable departures of the restructure, which was hastened by COVID, in as socially responsible a way as we could. Ninety-nine percent of all affected accepted voluntary agreements," Hallmark said. In reflection, he considers management's open and trustworthy approach as the key factor in securing a motivated workforce for the future of the company, as well as in handling this respectfully and silently, as it happened. There probably has been no better manifestation of the company's culture than at that time. Hallmark describes Bentley as "a family; it's quite humble. People would say we aim to be the best at what we do—looking after each other to create the best for our customers."

Preparation is key to protecting your business.

While Hallmark was pleasantly surprised by the Brexit preparations when he arrived, in hindsight they were only a quarter of the way toward what needed to be managed.

A cross-functional team was put together assuming a hard Brexit. One of the most critical decisions right at the start was to invest in initially three (and later five) times more warehousing capacity in order to keep more production parts in stock in case of disruption in supply. The single-digit million cost per year was much easier to digest compared to losing a month of sales, which would have created a negative impact of three-digit millions in revenues and two-digit millions in terms of profit. It was a true protection strategy.

Take a "calmly paranoid" approach.

"We assumed the worst case," Hallmark said, and in the context of COVID-19 that meant taking the responsibility for the lives of their workforce as seriously as possible. The approach Bentley took proved right. Not a single employee contracted the virus on the Bentley site—Hallmark remembered one client who picked up his new car during a non-lockdown period: "This gentleman had been hospitalized and said to our team, 'I feel safer here than in the hospital.'"

Continuously apply a "lessons learned" attitude.

"When COVID-19 hit, we built on the processes we had developed to deal with Brexit. Technically it makes no difference whether parts can't come in because of border controls or pandemic lockdowns," Hallmark said. But it was not just the flow of materials and products. First and foremost, this was about health. "Protect yourself, protect your colleagues, protect the family, and protect the business" is the mantra by which the company has operated since March 2020.

Involve all your stakeholders.

The automotive business is very much supplier and retailer heavy. Success depends on having them in the tent. In the case of Brexit, that meant that they would know, understand, and apply the revised processes to ensure that the business could operate with little to no disruption. The results were overwhelming. The business was able to operate without any closures—which would have been likely if the preparations had not been as solid and the partners had not been as on board as they were.

Bypass business as usual.

For decades, Dover was the harbor that all exports had to go through. Tests had shown it would be the bottleneck. So, securing capacities in Ipswich and Harwich before others would be able to do it was key. Again, questioning everything is an approach that pays off when uncertainty hits. Hiring 747 cargo aircraft for "shipping" new cars perfectly embodied the conviction to go the extra mile to keep the business afloat in the eyes of the industry and the proud Bentley customers who would receive their new cars on time.

**Understand your responsibility in a
"live or die" environment.**

Hallmark reflected on the impact of COVID-19 to him as a leader: "I have never worked before in an environment where your team could die as a result of coming to work. 2020 has been the most profound period of my working life." In a situation like this, there is not only the ethical responsibility but also the legal responsibility as a director of a business to the well-being and safety of one's workforce, and there is no question that those responsibilities weigh heavily on anyone who carries the privilege of corporate leadership.

Act with speed.

"We saw what happened with the pandemic in other European countries like Italy and chose to act significantly earlier before governmental decisions forced companies to take action," Hallmark said. This decision led to sourcing personal protection equipment from China well before the government did and applying a testing strategy for every member of the workforce at least once a week very early on. A "track and trace" system supported the approach; if anybody on-site discovered a risk area, they could note it via an app, and management had to deal with it within two hours. The company also supported delivering food or provisions for families that had COVID-19 cases.

> Hallmark reflected on the impact of COVID-19 to him as a leader: "I have never worked before in an environment where your team could die as a result of coming to work. 2020 has been the most profound period of my working life."

Hallmark summarized Bentley's efforts: "Open communication really does the trick. We have transformed our company into an inspired community. Openness, trust, and clarity are the building blocks of this success. These past three years despite all the challenges have been the most rewarding during my professional career." The numbers don't lie: Between 2018 and 2020, engagement and satisfaction scores among employees in the internal pulse surveys have grown from 72 percent to 85 percent. Every expert suggests numbers above 60 percent are good and anything above 70 percent is very good, but above 80 percent is a rare exception. With these scores, the people at Bentley can focus on their mission "to inspire our customers with a magical fusion of craftsmanship, innovation, and sustainability" and stay true to their vision "to create extraordinary journeys for customers." Good times ahead!

Seeking More Meaningful Workplace Experiences

At Bentley Motors, the workforce has lived through really challenging times. The values of innovation and sustainability, but foremost, authenticity, integrity, and collaboration, were tested like never before. The workforce became invigorated through the shared behaviors that were reinforced during these critical years. Bentley is a true role model in a world where today's job seekers are actively looking at companies' cultures and values over other employment factors, including salary.

A 2019 study by Glassdoor, the global website that offers employees the opportunity to share reviews of their experience at their company anonymously to the benefit of job seekers (and actually employers who want to improve their employer brand by actions and not just words), shows the shift in what matters when individuals are seeking a new job. Their Mission & Culture Survey[64] revealed that more than 77 percent of adults across four countries (the United States, the United Kingdom, France, Germany) would consider a company's culture before applying for a job there, and 79 percent would consider a company's mission and purpose before applying. Furthermore, over half of the 5,000 respondents said that company culture is more important than salary when it comes to job satisfaction. What a shift—it used to be high salaries, the company car, basically anything that falls under "compensation and benefits." Today, this category only counts for 12 percent, whereas "culture and values" counts for 22 percent, nearly twice as much.

After the study's release, Christian Sutherland-Wong, Glassdoor president and COO, commented: "Across the countries we surveyed, it's clear that job seekers are seeking more meaningful workplace experiences. They want to be paid fairly but they too want to work for a company whose values align with their own and whose mission they can fully get behind."[65]

- - - - - - - - - - -

64, 65   https://about-content.glassdoor.com/en-us/workplace-culture-over-salary/

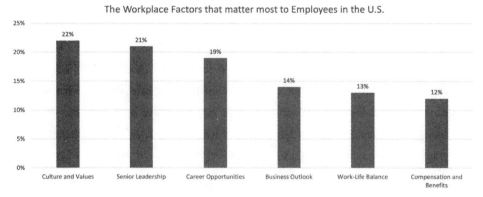

The Workplace Factors that matter most to Employees in the U.S.

Source: Glassdoor Economic Research (Glassdoor.com/Research).

Figure 8: Glassdoor study on workplace culture over salary.

The Glassdoor study data represents all job seekers. The younger the individuals get, the more culture and values matter. Millennials and younger adults in the United States and United Kingdom are more likely to prioritize culture above salary. According to Glassdoor's chief economist, Dr. Andrew Chamberlain, "A common misperception among many employers today is that pay and work-life balance are among the top factors driving employee satisfaction. We find little support for this notion in Glassdoor data. Instead, employers looking to boost recruiting and retention efforts should prioritize building strong company culture and value systems, amplifying the quality and visibility of their senior leadership teams and offering clear, exciting career opportunities to employees."[66]

The survey also found that 73 percent of all adults surveyed would not apply to a company unless its values aligned with their own personal values, and 89 percent believe it is important for an employer to have a clear mission and purpose—and that is nearly the same number across all countries surveyed. Seventy-nine percent would consider a company's mission

----

66   https://about-content.glassdoor.com/en-us/workplace-culture-over-salary/

before applying for a job there, demonstrating just how important a clear mission is to recruitment. Sixty-six percent of employees believe people are more motivated and engaged because of the strong company mission where they work, and 64 percent say their company's mission is one of the main reasons they stay in their job. Opinions do differ by country, however: Employees in France are more likely than in any other country to say their company's mission is one of the main reasons they stay in their job (70 percent vs. 60 percent in the United Kingdom, 64 percent in the United States, and 63 percent in Germany).

Glassdoor's Big Nine

Donald Sull, a senior lecturer at the MIT Sloan School of Management, breaks down the important elements of company culture based on research from Glassdoor and MIT: "When we talk about culture, we have a very specific definition of culture. We are talking about a bundle of values and norms that are deeply held by people, widely shared throughout the organization that shape behavior over time."[67]

In a study MIT did for Glassdoor, results showed that 96 percent of all Glassdoor reviews are about some element of culture. Nine values—"the Big Nine"—have emerged from this research. Sull has developed a tool, called the "Culture 500," that allows him to compare corporate cultures of more than 500 top US companies based on more than 1.2 million Glassdoor reviews. Across thirty-one categories, these corporations employ a quarter of the private sector. For the first time, there is a tool to compare companies within the same category. It creates an understanding of how they are doing in reality compared to their peers against the Big Nine values. The MIT researchers used a natural language–processing algorithm to classify free text into more than eighty culture-related topics; those were then categorized into nine cultural values.

- - - - - - - - - - -

67   https://www.youtube.com/watch?v=q7F4AxyGDAA

Value	Definition
Agility	Companies are nimble, flexible, and quick to seize opportunities.
Collaboration	Employees stay cohesive and productive within their groups and across teams.
Customer	Companies prioritize customers' needs and focus on creating value for them.
Diversity	Companies emphasize building inclusive cultures.
Execution	Companies foster behaviors like being accountable for results, delivering on commitments, and adhering to a discipline process.
Innovation	Companies fuel creativity and experimentation and are eager to implement new ideas.
Integrity	Employees across the board maintain a code of honesty and ethics that consistently inform their actions.
Performance	Companies recognize performance and reward results through compensation, recognition, and promotion, as well as handling underperforming employees tactfully and strategically.
Respect	Employees, managers, and leaders treat one another with dignity and take one another's perspectives seriously.

Table 2: MIT / Glassdoor nine key values—"The Big Nine."

Glassdoor stated that this algorithm allows job seekers to "customize their searches by pulling a set of companies and comparing them along any of the Big Nine values. The Culture 500 systematizes cultural analysis for companies and for job seekers alike. It makes the abstract tangible, inviting informed conversations about culture, which benefit those on both sides of the table." Here are the Big Nine values:[68]

- - - - - - - - - - -

68   https://www.glassdoor.com/employers/blog/what-aspects-of-company-culture-matter-most-in-todays-job-economy/

Corporate Culture Myths

Glassdoor's Donald Sull also has looked at corporate culture myths throughout his career and has come to define five key myths.[69]

Myth 1: "You can really rely on gut feel." When you just believe your own jargon and your own press statements, you start detaching yourself from the organization. It is so critical to understand what is going on—not just what you want to be going on.

Myth 2: "Declaring official values is enough." In his view, behaviors form culture more than any written statements—hence the Soul System™ involves the relationship between shared understanding and shared behavior.

Myth 3: "Culture eats strategy for lunch." Whether it is breakfast or lunch . . . he argues that both matter and both need to be aligned. That is the hardest thing to achieve as it touches every aspect of the corporation.

Myth 4: "Change values to change behaviors." I have come across this one many, many times. From his point of view, behaviors show the values of the company—hence managing the behaviors in the desired way is far more critical than writing up just another value statement.

Myth 5: "You can change culture without changing people." This one is the toughest: Often leaders shy away from letting managers go who have a toxic effect on the culture. Putting those people through reorientation workshops and training hardly ever works. If you have tried and you are honest with yourself, you will agree that this is a real myth. I have never seen it happen. And it is clear: If behaviors drive values (myth 4), then people need to be able to really change behavior to change culture. If there are serious doubts about individuals and their ability to do so, you have to be prepared to make the tough decisions.

Understanding your company's soul is critical for the success of yourself as a leader and for the success of your company. Be sure you have a shared purpose in place with a shared understanding of your company's vision, mission, values, and spirit that allows for the shared behaviors that

----

69   https://www.youtube.com/watch?v=q7F4AxyGDAA

make corporate soul come to life in the eyes of your associates, as well as your customers and all other stakeholders.

Key thoughts to consider on
understanding your company's soul

	Soul Searching in Action
✓	Are you able to define the culture of your company in one sentence?
✓	Would your management team use the same words on their own?
✓	Have you coded your company's soul through events and activities?
✓	Does your staff survey allow associates to evaluate the meaningfulness of their workplace?
✓	Is your employer branding in sync with the real culture of your workplace?
✓	What role does empathy play in leadership behaviors?
✓	Are you prepared to change people when you need to change culture?
✓	Is your leadership team visible and approachable to all?

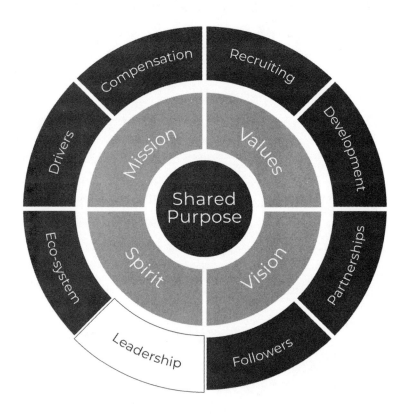

Figure 9: Leadership as a critical component within shared behaviors of the Soul System™.

CHAPTER 5

Lead with Soul

How can you reinforce the soul of your company
at every level of your leadership structure?

Chapter Goal:

- - - - - - - - - - - - -

Create a culture where everyone feels your support
when they act according to your company's shared
behaviors—and where everyone understands that each
of your actions reinforces the corporate soul every day.

The larger your company becomes, the more challenges will be
around the corner to ensure the soul of your company stays
healthy. Your first twenty associates will get it from the horse's
mouth every day and reinforcing the soul of the company will be a natural
thing. But then, if your product and your business model are sound, the
company will grow and you will need to establish larger leadership structures. I remember when we built Spark44, there was a very critical moment
that almost killed our corporate soul. In 2015 we tripled the size of the

business in just six months. We took the company from 250 people to 750 and moved from 6 to 16 offices in just a few weeks. One of our clients warned us when we were creating the plan that we would be a different company after this. He was right and wrong at the same time. He was wrong since the founders were still on board and had a close eye on ensuring the culture that had been built was fostered. But he was also right: Bringing in new employees in a 2:1 ratio to the existing ones created many challenging situations. New joiners who had previously worked for the same client in a different agency said, "We have always done it this way with this client," but our approach to managing similar situations was quite different. Unlearning behaviors that might have been recognized in a different environment is critical when it comes to ensuring your company's soul is not weakened. The sheer volume of new people was also a big challenge.

> Unlearning behaviors that might have been recognized in a different environment is critical when it comes to ensuring your company's soul is not weakened.

When I discussed the potential issues of our growth plan with my board colleagues, I was optimistic—because I knew the leadership potential we had in our people who served as client liaisons via an associated hub office in the markets where we did not have a full agency. I knew that the people who already had been with us for two years were fully on board. They were clear about our purpose; they knew our values. For our ten new offices, we were able to promote eight of our local people to the position of general manager. Two had to be hired—through an extensive interviewing and referencing process to ensure they would be a good fit. One of them turned out to be a rock star, who got it immediately. The other one was a complete mistake and had to be replaced within weeks. Even with the best interviews, it is not easy to make the right decisions—at least our "early-warning system" worked. But nine out of ten was a pretty good ratio that allowed us to evangelize to our new five hundred hires with the spirit that we wanted to feel when we came to the office every morning. Our corporate soul remained intact.

Spark44's staff growth was immense for a firm of its size—but still a different kettle of fish when you compare it to an S&P 500–sized company. While the principles are the same, the execution is much more critical. One cannot underestimate the effort it takes, but I can assure you it is worth it. No matter which industry you operate in, promoting a shared understanding of your company's shared purpose drives your shared behaviors across the firm, but it is definitely making a difference in the service industry. There are two great examples—Salesforce in the area of customer engagement and Hilton in the hospitality space.

Ohana Means Family. Family Means Nobody Gets Left Behind—Or Forgotten.

Similar to how Adrian Hallmark talks about the "Bentley family," so too does Marc Benioff, the founder of Salesforce. When you listen to him, you get a strong sense of how all-encompassing he believes the culture is for his company. He introduced the word Ohana, which is a word that is part of the Hawaiian language—he considers his place in Hawaii a second home. It is a term that was chosen wisely—the company is in the business of customer relationship management (CRM). I once came across a CRM consultant who I asked for the simplest definition of what he is trying to achieve with his programs. His reply: "Remember me." That is still the best definition of what a good CRM program does that I have come across. And "Remember me" is another way to express what Ohana means—nobody gets left behind.

During one of Benioff's sessions with his leadership team, he explained what Ohana really means.[70] "Look, this is our culture, this is our family," he said. "But our family is also our customers, and our partners are our family. Our Ohana is not just our employees in this room. We have a very big and growing Ohana. I look at it that way: I say to our employees, 'You treat our customers the way you treat your family.' That's the behavior we

----

70   https://www.youtube.com/watch?v=1_4rHKGHImU

want. You treat the partners the way you treat your family. And if that isn't the way you are doing it, then we are not being Salesforce. Because that's how Salesforce behaves."

In Salesforce's Ohana corporate video, the firm overtly used the word soul: "We are talking about a company that's got one of the greatest corporate souls." Benioff is quoted as saying, "I am running a company based on stakeholders, not shareholders."[71] Quite a successful company, as media quotes such as "Salesforce dominates CRM" or "Most innovative company in the world" (both from Forbes) appear on the screen while the corporate culture is portrayed.

Equality and Diversity

Leadership values as part of the company's shared behaviors are critical. Ideally, leaders are role models for an organization. At Salesforce, two key leadership values are equality and diversity. To improve equality, the company made a commitment in 2015 to equal pay for men and women. On its website, Salesforce updates its equality efforts regularly. Have a look at this Salesforce statement from 2019: "We've completed our fourth companywide equal pay assessment, which found that 5% of our 35,000 employees globally required adjustments. Of those who required adjustments, 39% were women, 54% were men, and 7% were due to race and ethnicity. As a result, the company spent $1.6 million to make those adjustments. To date, Salesforce has spent a total of $10.3 million to ensure equal pay for equal work."[72] Benioff takes equality seriously, hence he elevated Tony Prophet, who joined the firm in 2016 to lead the office of equality, to the C-suite in 2020 as the chief equality and recruiting officer. If you Google "chief equality officer," the first page shows you only mentions of Tony's name. In an interview with

----

71   https://www.youtube.com/watch?v=AJu_wtnXXa4
72   https://www.salesforce.com/blog/2019/04/equal-pay-update-2019.html

Diginomica,[73] he discussed why the company is pioneering in this work: "All the things that are happening in society and all the issues that come up where their customers and their employees and their stakeholders are asking them—where do you stand?" It has taken many decades for chief equality officer positions to appear in the boardrooms. Just in February 2021, the US State Department introduced the position of a chief diversity officer to make the diplomatic corps more representative of the various backgrounds of the country.

As part of its diversity efforts, Salesforce provides leaders of a team of five hundred or more with a monthly scorecard to create visibility on how often they promote and hire women and underrepresented minorities. Staff at Salesforce consists of one-third women and two-thirds men. Senior leaders receive their scorecard detailing the headcount, hiring, attrition, and promotion data by gender (global) and race (United States). The company's largest organizations are guided by an Equality Board made up of their recruiting, employee success, equality partners, and senior leaders to drive prescriptive actions based on data. This is not just an anecdotal approach to have fig-leaf solutions, but instead has become a truly data-driven exercise that covers all areas of the approximately 50,000-person company.

Salesforce's vision statement takes the high ground: "We believe that the business of business is to improve the state of the world, and we work to make sure Salesforce is a platform for change through serving the interests of all our stakeholders—employees, customers, partners, communities and the environment."[74]

While Salesforce is a 50,000-employee company, Spark44 was an agency with 19 offices and 1,200 people at its peak. The very lean leadership structure did not require a scorecard—I was able to name every managing director without a huge organizational chart. When we went through our

----

73   https://diginomica.com/salesforces-chief-equality-officer-asks-which-side-of-history-do-you-want-to-be-on

74   https://www.salesforce.com/company/sustainability/vision/

accelerated growth period, I was very proud when we counted our male/female ratio among our managing directors and it was exactly 50/50.

In an *AdAge* interview[75] about diversity, Britton Jonathan Jackson, Spark44's director of production for the North American offices in New York and Toronto, spoke about how Spark44's diversity and equality efforts created an atmosphere where people wanted to come to work:

> I manage a team of 11 people across both offices: NYC and Toronto. I joined Spark44 a little over four years ago after being at MRM/McCann for 8-plus years. At the time I was looking for a change of both company and client to help expand my career and diversify my experience. Over the years, I had kept in touch with my colleague and friend Sabina Sebastian, whom I had worked with early on at MRM/McCann and was the business director at Spark44. I really respected her and how she moved her career along. She told me that Spark44 was looking for a senior print producer.
>
> When I came into the office for my interview, I was pleasantly surprised. Not only was the luxury auto brand exactly what I wanted to round out my experience, but the office was the most diverse I had seen in my 15-plus years in advertising. Sabina herself is Indian-American. The managing director at the time, Tony Hobley was Black, in addition to the other people of color that I saw in different roles throughout this mid-sized agency. I knew this was where I wanted to work immediately. By seeing people of color in high-level positions, I knew that there existed a possibility of a level playing field for growth—something that is rare in this industry. I was able to go from a senior print producer to team leader and now the Director of Production.

----

75   https://adage.com/article/agency-news/uncomfortable-conversations-importance-black-mentorship/2266236

Recruitment Is the Number One Job for Leaders

In 2017, Hilton CEO Christopher Nassetta earned the forty-ninth spot on the Employees' Choice Award for Highest-Rated CEOs at Glassdoor. The Glassdoor team interviewed Hilton's chief human resources officer, Matthew Schuyler, to understand what got the company there. The Glassdoor team asked what the company does specifically to foster employee trust and engagement.[76]

"We believe the number one job of our leaders is to recruit great talent," Schuyler replied. "Once you recruit great talent, then introducing them through the recruitment process and ultimately the onboarding process, the strategy, the mission, the vision, the priorities of company, our values is where leadership sort of kicks in. Recruit and then motivate through our shared values and purpose. Our purpose in short is really about hospitality. We believe it's our mission to be the most hospitable company in the world. To deliver on our original founder's—our namesake's goal is to spread the light and warmth of that hospitality around the world. That is the higher calling, the purpose that we rally our teams around and ask our leaders to be spokespeople for—and it sort of starts from there."

From there, Schuyler discussed the most important elements when it comes to recruiting leaders: "We do a lot to develop our leaders and our managers. We have a very defined curriculum that we both encourage our leaders to work their way through and in some instances mandate that they go through in order to make it to the next level."

He went on to describe how Hilton's formal annual global team member survey is completed by the majority of all employees—90 percent in 2019. Those hundreds of thousands of data points allow the firm to build its Leadership Index, which gives Hilton's leaders and managers scores relative to how they're doing in the eyes of the team around them. Said Schuyler, "We're measuring things like what is the morale of your team?

----

76 https://www.glassdoor.com/employers/blog/how-hilton-manages-its-global-enterprise-for-great-leadership/

Are they engaged in their work? Do they feel good about where the company is heading? Do they feel good about you as a leader? Do they feel like they are looked after for their next career move? Do they feel like they can be themselves at work? Is this an inclusive work environment?"

Many companies run team surveys and leadership surveys. But very often they live a life of their own—in the closet. Done, shared, filed—period. But at Hilton, the results of its annual survey become part of the bonus cycle of every leader. This continuous feedback cycle of asking for and receiving feedback on how its leaders are doing helps them to become better leaders—and drives behaviors across the firm in the direction of the company's shared behaviors.

Leadership Principles Need to Be Clear for Everyone

During my leadership experiences, I have come across many leaders who believe they lead with soul, but in the eyes of those they were leading, that was not the case. Some mixed up leading with *their* soul with leading along the lines of the *company soul*—but in reality the two souls were not aligned. Others felt that they were leading with soul but nobody except themselves was able to recognize it.

As we previously discussed, a shared purpose is key to building corporate soul. The 2017 EY study "How Can Purpose Reveal a Path through Disruption?"[77] provides a quantitative lens to the importance of purpose. While *purpose* has become the buzzword in the management theory debate, the reality shows that there are significant gaps between what is written in powerful statements and what is the everyday reality in offices around the world. Nearly 1,500 senior executives and business leaders from around the world participated. Parallel research with

----

77   https://assets.ey.com/content/dam/ey-sites/ey-com/en_gl/topics/purpose/purpose-pdfs/
       ey-how-can-purpose-reveal-a-path-through-uncertainty.pdf

lower- and middle-level managers balanced the study. The top-line summary: "Executives significantly overrated how well their employees experienced their firm's purpose. Executives think their firms are truly purpose-driven, but their employees disagree."

The red thread across the study is the requirement for "Engaged Leadership" to build purpose-driven businesses. One quote of a participant says it all: "You need to have a CEO who lives and breathes [their purpose] every day." But the reality is different. The EY research and observations suggest leaders may often be a casualty of a pervasive overconfidence bias that leaves them viewing their company's commitment to purpose far more optimistically than their employees do. Research by EY and Forbes Insights in their "Is Your Purpose Lectured, or Lived?" study[78] found that the more senior an executive, the more confident they are of both articulation and activation of purpose within their firm. Ninety-eight percent of CEOs surveyed agreed with the statement that "our purpose is central to our organization and is well understood by all." But this confidence progressively weakened at each lower level of management, falling to 50 percent among vice presidents. A similar pattern held when respondents were asked to what extent purpose determined their firm's strategy and decision-making. The same study suggests that "many workers believe their organization's broader purpose hasn't been properly explained to them. Far fewer employees believed that their organization had a purpose focused on multiple stakeholders than did senior executives. Workers were much more likely to state that their company's purpose was purely to create value for customers—something those on the front lines were more used to hearing."

The Reputation Risk

"Tell the audience what you are going to say, say it; then tell them what you've said." Dale Carnegie's tip for successful presentations is still key—no

- - - - - - - - - - -

78   https://www.ey.com/en_gl/purpose/is-your-purpose-lectured-or-lived

wonder, as this universal thought had been first put down on paper by the famous Greek philosopher Aristotle. Leaders need to inhale those words—but words are not enough. Once you "tell them what you've said," then you must do what you told them you would do. This is critical for the credibility of leaders. In other words, the right *behavior* is required to ensure employees do not feel a "say–do" gap.

It is obvious that these gaps are a reality. Look at approval rates on Glassdoor for various companies and you can see it. Even if you discount the bias of unhappy leavers and accept a share of employees who don't really engage, there are still lots of companies where data shows a significant gap compared to the spirit CEOs convey in their speeches. Yet these speeches are critical. The "Is Your Purpose Lectured, or Lived?" study confirms that loud and clear: "Leading companies clearly articulate why their firm exists. What do they stand for? What makes it worth their employees giving their time—the most valuable asset they have? Rather than stopping there, businesses that live their purpose drive that message home by demonstrating how it is connected to what the business actually does commercially. Are its strategies supporting its purpose? Or is it just growth for the sake of growth, profits for the sake of profits? If a purpose is truly to take hold, it needs to be *repeated* and *reinforced* continuously by leaders at all levels of the organization."

Since every employee is not just a stakeholder but also a multiplier in terms of the reputation of the enterprise or brand, the risk for the company of a badly managed purpose is high. Customers and other stakeholders receive mixed messages—a real issue in the era of social media. The same EY study states a significant disconnect on the employee experience of purpose. Senior leaders on average rate that employee experience at a level of 63%. Employees themselves consider that level only to reach 47%. A 16 percentage points gap. This underlines the importance of the word *shared* when it comes to purpose statements—as well as the corresponding shared understanding and shared behavior.

The Business Opportunity

While this risk is immense, on the other hand the opportunity is, too. The EY study "Is Your Purpose Lectured, or Lived?" defines purposeful companies as "those that go beyond share-holder profits to encompass a purpose that serves employees, customers and society as a whole (purpose with a 'capital P'). Purposeful companies successfully drive their purpose into their organizations and recognize the importance of truly engaging their employ-ees on the firm's purpose journey." EY's research shows that these companies are bet-ter at attracting talent, spurring innovation, navigating disruption, and, yes, making a profit—all key for surviving and thriving in today's volatile world. Getting it right provides powerful rewards—execu-tion of the Soul System™ in creating a shared understanding and aligned behaviors is worth the effort. It does not just make everybody feel better, but it also pays off. Or, as the EY study puts it, "As leaders of some of the world's leading companies are finding, an organizational purpose that goes beyond quarterly profits and shareholder dividends isn't just good for morale—it's good for business."

> Getting it right provides powerful rewards— execution of the Soul System™ in creating a shared understanding and aligned behaviors is worth the effort. It does not just make everybody feel better, but it also pays off.

Many employees still think of their jobs in terms of immediate tasks rather than the larger, aspirational purpose for which executives claim the organization exists. In these cases, business leaders have failed to convey how the broader purpose relates to the work of the employees, resulting in an absence of resonance and buy-in.

US-based consultancy Gapingvoid Culture Design Group did a remarkable piece of analysis on this problem. In March 2020, they published their study "Culture as a Management System: How CEOs Who Lead High-Purpose Organizational Cultures Deliver Remarkable

Business Performance."[79] It focuses on businesses with high-purpose cultures—those that are both employee- and customer-focused. These businesses walk the talk through their decisions and actions, not just through statements. According to the Gapingvoid study, "When a business aligns around a high-purpose culture, employees know it." Gapingvoid CEO and cofounder Jason Korman has seen how Glassdoor results can serve as a powerful sign of whether any given company has a high-purpose culture: "To be among Glassdoor's best-rated companies, a business must be popular with employees. And as Glassdoor's study shows, employees rank culture as the most important factor in determining their satisfaction."

The Gapingvoid analysis established that businesses with high-purpose cultures beat competition: "They experience higher financial returns, better customer satisfaction scores, increased employee retention, greater innovation, and greater competitive advantage."

The Gapingvoid research also shows that there is a significant benefit for CEOs themselves, stating, "When they successfully implement these kinds of cultures, CEOs receive higher compensation as a percentage of corporate revenue. They also get greater numbers of positive media mentions. And they experience increased respect by employees and communities, as often indicated by their presence on lists of the most admired CEOs." That uplift in compensation can be considerable as the Gapingvoid study shows: "The CEOs we analyzed who instill and oversee high-purpose cultures earned total compensation of about 0.16% of company revenues. At the other end of the spectrum, CEOs from companies with poor culture scores, overseeing low-purpose cultures, earned about 0.07% of total revenues."

Ultimately, as Gapingvoid's Korman highlights, "Well-designed cultures act as management systems that work to ensure consistent organizational outcomes. Having spent more than a decade working with businesses across numerous sectors to help them build these kinds of cultures, I've seen the night-and-day difference they can make."

- - - - - - - - - - - -

79   https://www.gapingvoid.com/ceo-culture-study

A New Framework Emerges

Seymour Burchman, who is a managing director at Semler Brossy—an independent executive compensation consulting firm founded in 2001—has consulted on executive pay and leadership performance for over forty S&P 500 companies. He knows what has changed over the years since he has been in this business for over thirty years. He mapped the relevant changes in an article that was published in the *Harvard Business Review* in February 2020 titled "A Framework for Executive Compensation"[80] comparing the standard incentive design today versus tomorrow.

Today	Tomorrow	Rationale
Strategy-driven	Mission/purpose-driven	More enduring and flexible
Shareholder-centric	Stakeholder-centric	Broader focus to reflect mission
Strategic milestone-focused	Stakeholder outcome-focused	Consistent, longer-term focus
Financial goals primarily	Financial and nonfinancial goals	Better aligned with mission/stakeholder outcomes
Overlapping independent cycles	End-to-end cycles, using the same outcome measures for each cycle	Longer-term focus, avoiding contradictory annual goals
Budgeted performance	Goals that improve: (1) at a set amount over prior cycle and (2) relative to peer performance	More enduring over time while avoiding tie to strategic plans

Table 3: Seymour Burchman comparison of the standard incentive design today versus tomorrow—The Evolution to a New Standard in Long-Term Incentive Pay.

----

80   https://hbr.org/2020/02/a-new-framework-for-executive-compensation

"Long-term" is the guiding principle. You could also name it "more sustainable." This does not come as a surprise. The 2018 McKinsey study "Disruptive Forces in the Industrial Sectors"[81] looked into the automotive, electronics, aerospace, and defense industries and concluded that "the industrial sectors will see more disruption within the next five years than in the past 20 years combined." Accenture came to similar conclusions in its "Breaking through Disruption" study.[82] In its 2019 Disruptability Index 2.0, Accenture analyzed how the nature of disruption evolved between 2011 and 2018 for eighteen industry sectors. The conclusion was straightforward: "Our longitudinal research reveals that industry disruption is a persistent condition—not short-lived."

This is where Burchman sees the need for action. He writes, "The responses to this disruption . . . have not been matched in long-term incentive design. Conventional plans reward executives for winning over three years. Because companies now are vying to reshape their business over much longer periods, executives are essentially tied to a structure that supports only incremental change versus radical transformation. This disconnect means a clash is inevitable. The solution to the disconnect is not obvious, because the search for new plan designs poses an apparent riddle: How do you set goals for long-term transformation, short-term strategic agility, and the building of stakeholder ecosystems all at the same time? Doesn't that require irreconcilable tradeoffs?"[83]

In Burchman's view there is a way to avoid these potentially irreconcilable trade-offs. He suggests that companies let their mission guide them:

> Your company's mission offers consistent, yet flexible, guidance
> for long-term transformation, agile course corrections, and the

---

81   https://www.mckinsey.com/industries/automotive-and-assembly/our-insights/disruptive-trends-that-will-transform-the-auto-industry

82   https://www.accenture.com/_acnmedia/Thought-Leadership-Assets/PDF/Accenture-Breaking-Through-Disruption-Embrace-the-Power-of-the-Wise-Pivot

83   https://hbr.org/2020/02/a-new-framework-for-executive-compensation

building, operation, and constant reshaping of stakeholder-rich ecosystems. For effective guidance, a mission needs to answer specific questions that can be translated into long-term, measurable goals:

- *Who or what* are we benefiting?

- What *stakeholder outcomes* are required to create that benefit?

- How can we *continuously improve* those outcomes—and *outperform* competitors?

This approach fits the thinking behind the Gapingvoid study extremely well. Compensation and incentive systems for management need to be linked, with the company's purpose and mission being long-term and serving multiple stakeholders.

Everything Communicates

"The more people you're responsible for, the more your words and the way you communicate those words and your body language and essentially everything you do is taken into consideration by the team."[84] This quote from LinkedIn's Jeff Weiner embodies what *leading with soul* means. In an interview with *Business Insider*,[85] Weiner elaborated on this topic: "You have to be that much more aware of the way in which you're coming across. And I think the best leaders maintain awareness of their environment and in real time can course correct. It doesn't matter if they're in a one-on-one, or a staff meeting, in an all-hands session, or speaking to thousands of people at a keynote. They are always aware of the way they

----

84   https://www.linkedin.com/pulse/linkedin-ceo-jeff-weiner-describes-3-qualities-make-great-kojouri/

85   https://www.businessinsider.com/linkedin-ceo-jeff-weiner-on-leadership-2014-9

are being received. They can course correct so they can ensure that what they're saying is resonating and that it's bringing people together."

It is the way you speak; it is the medium that you choose; it is the selection of people that you bring together—it really is everything. And then it is, of course, what you say, or better, what you have to say. This is true for everyone in a leadership position—and many are not aware of it.

In his wonderful book about emotional intelligence, *The Case of the Missing Cutlery*,[86] Kevin Allen starts his introduction this way: "Well, kid, welcome to the club. You are now dinner conversation." He refers here to good advice he received from one of his mentors at Marriott International after being promoted into his first management role at the age of twenty-two: Your staff will now be talking about you. So the choice is yours—what do you want people who have been part of your working day to say about you? In the context of the corporate soul, what is it that you want to be connected with? In Jeff Weiner's case where personal vision and company vision feel extremely in sync, the employees get that the company's focus and Weiner's own focus are the same. You do not get a 100 percent rating on Glassdoor if it is not.

Great Leaders Can Help Others to Become Great Leaders

When we founded Spark44, I felt it was vitally important to establish a means by which we could both motivate and measure our people, providing them with a constant source of feedback and the guidance to grow in their jobs. Our first chairman, Hans Riedel, played a critical role in this—his experience as the former Porsche global sales and marketing director, as well as his agency background with Young & Rubicam, was vital. He combined both a client and an agency background, which enabled him to balance the needs of either party of the joint venture. His understanding of the

----

86   Kevin Allen. *The Case of the Missing Cutlery.* New York: Bibliomotion, 2014.

importance of building and managing teams was priceless. Based on Riedel's input and a variety of expert essays, our first CEO Steve Woolford recommended introducing a process of quarterly evaluations. We would dedicate ourselves to a process of two-way feedback for each and every person in the organization, including myself. This ran counter to the typical annual evaluation or even the total absence in many places of any evaluations, but conducting evaluations frequently through the year provided a pathway for the growth of our people.

> We very quickly figured out that we would do ourselves a big favor if we didn't separate the evaluations by profession, competency, or capability, but actually connected them with the values that we wanted the business to represent.

Initially the evaluations were designed separately for each department, like creative or strategy. We very quickly figured out that we would do ourselves a big favor if we didn't separate the evaluations by profession, competency, or capability, but actually connected them with the values that we wanted the business to represent. In constructing this program, it became all too clear to me why programs of this kind are not implemented. It takes an enormous amount of time and energy. Imagine doing this with about twenty people—half an hour each and ten hours in a quarter is a day or, let's say, two days with preparation and with follow-ups. Multiply this by four times a year and you get quite a commitment. We were convinced, however, that this—not managing granularity—was the true role of management, so we embarked on a commitment to explore a quarterly program.

We linked the evaluative criteria to our corporate values of *be bold, be brave,* and *be honest,* with ten specific evaluative criteria for each professional department. We measured everybody against those on a scale from 1 to 5. It was a rolling process, with the current quarter's evaluation becoming the basis for the next quarter's evaluations. We built a "stop-continue-start" logic of counseling:

STOP: That's not so great; why don't you stop doing that?
CONTINUE: Continue doing that. That's great!
START: Hey, why don't you start doing that?

The program went through the entire agency from a new employee to the CEO. Everybody was evaluated. The effect was utterly transformative. Rather than a punitive, or "putting people on the griddle," type of affair, it became a pep rally, providing people with rolling motivational feedback to help them become greater than they believed they were. We let them know how brilliant they were but how much more effective they could be.

In the beginning, we did this with Excel spreadsheets because it was just twenty people per office. So not a big deal. As we grew, we moved into a software solution with ClearCompany, which specialized in doing these online evaluations. They customized the system for us, and Spark44 has been operating with it ever since.

ClearCompany's CEO and cofounder, Andre Lavoie, provided an overview in 2015 about five strategies that are vital to developing employee leadership skills, and all of them are right on the money:[87]

1. Encourage employees to network.

2. Act as a mentor (or assign one).

3. Provide opportunities for growth.

4. Maintain a feedback loop.

5. Lead by example.

"Employee development isn't just the responsibility of the employee, but of the employer as well—if not more so," Lavoie writes. "Good managers strive to continuously groom their employees for future leadership roles. Doing so not only boosts employee engagement and productivity,

- - - - - - - - - - -

87   https://www.entrepreneur.com/article/242663

but it makes employers' lives a little easier, by making employee transitions into leadership roles as seamless as possible." We leveraged his five strategies as critical elements to create the framework of shared behaviors in our evaluation structure, which focused a great deal on values and behaviors.

Seventy percent of our evaluation score was based on values and behaviors; 30 percent was based on the achievement of annual goals for the individuals. Lavoie's first principle, "Encourage employees to network," was really critical to us. We called it "collaboration" and asked our people to score themselves between 1 and 5 against this notion: "Actively builds a wide range of alliances across boundaries, internally and externally. Actively strives to support and contribute to the output of the wider team and agency." This one alone did wonders in helping people understand their active role in making them a real part of a network.

The second principle, "Act as a mentor (or assign one)," was summarized under the idea of "boldness" by establishing the role of each individual as someone who "acts as an ambassador for their areas of the business and for our work." An element of the ambassador role was to ensure that mentors were identified and connected with their mentees.

Principle number three, "Provide opportunities for growth," was essential in building our learning and training program for all levels of the company. Each individual's needs were collected, and, on that basis, an annual training program for the entire company was tailored.

The fourth principle, "Maintain a feedback loop," was really critical as it ensured that the employee provided a self-assessment and the corresponding line manager discussed their feedback in the context of that self-assessment. It did lead to very interesting debates at times when both showed a significant gap in their views.

"Lead by example" is Lavoie's fifth principle. We decided that this one was so important that we actually included a number of questions around it within the evaluation. In "Bravery" we asked for a score regarding "Puts themselves forward for new challenges, steps outside their comfort zone." In "Empathy" the score related to "Demonstrates the ability to understand other people's emotions and how their own behavior can impact other people," and in "Proactive" we tried to understand (and evaluate) "Looks at problems from a whole new angle, thinking beyond the boundaries of their current role/tasks."

Leading by Example When You Go Public

In a 2014 *Business Insider* interview,[88] LinkedIn's Jeff Weiner was asked about how he felt during the ups of the company's IPO and the downs further down the line. His reply to Henry Blodget in response to a board member regarding the requirements of a public company versus a private one is a testament to the leadership qualities of someone who can lead with soul: "We're going to play up to who we aspire to be and not play down to the lowest common denominator out of fear of what might happen. As soon as you do that, it's done. . . . The street determines our day-to-day share price. We determine the long-term value."

His passion for key strategic pillars (vision, mission, values, culture) and the roadmap (i.e., operational long-term focus) along with transparency towards employees did not allow for anything to call them into question. Weiner simply wanted the company to remain the company he was proud of, even with a broader ownership basis. Trading values (being open, honest, and constructive) for non-transparency, as other companies do, was no option. His position of being risk-averse was proven right—the risk of putting the shared understanding and shared behavior of the company on the line was considered higher than a potential leak of confidential information given the tradition of transparency of the firm.

That is what I call leading with soul—being firm on the company's shared purpose and the corresponding shared understanding and shared behaviors, no matter what the pressures are. A similar consideration happened at Bentley Motors when CEO and Chairman Adrian Hallmark had to decide whether he would be totally open and transparent about the turnaround plan for the British carmaker (see chapter 4).

----

88   https://www.businessinsider.com/linkedin-ceo-jeff-weiner-on-leadership-2014-9

Key thoughts to consider on leading with soul

Soul Searching in Action
✓   Are your leadership principles clear for everyone?
✓   Do you help others to become great leaders?
✓   Are you conscious that everything you do and say (or not say) is interpreted by your peers and associates?
✓   Have you created a culture that supports everything that is in line with the shared behaviors?
✓   Do you rely on your gut feeling or do you measure actions against objectives?
✓   Do you offer recruitment candidates of the next two levels an opportunity to meet with you before the decision is made?
✓   Do your staff diversity ratios support your company's ambition in this space?
✓   Did you realize which of your actions today reinforced the corporate soul?

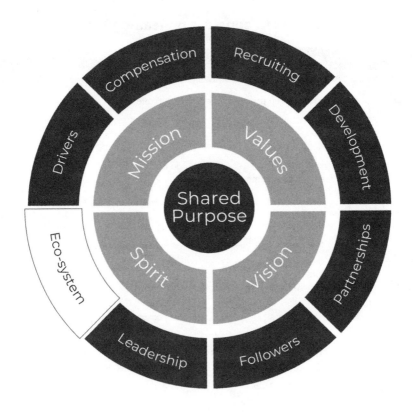

Figure 10: Soul ecosystem as a critical component within shared behaviors of the Soul System™.

CHAPTER 6

Nurture the Soul Ecosystem

Which are the elements that define the soul ecosystem?
What is needed to make it future-proof?

Chapter Goal:
- - - - - - - - - - - - - -

Manage what really matters through measurable objectives and
key results that are linked to your company's environmental,
social, and governance challenges and stand true to the changing
societies in which you operate.

S ouls are very sensitive. Individual souls, but also collective souls,
as in the soul of a company. As with individuals, companies go
through ups and downs. The resilience of their organization is a
testament to the ecosystem of all the players inside the organization and
the stakeholders outside the firm. The shared behaviors inside the company allow new employees to "get it" fast—actions speak louder than

words, and the behaviors display what gets rewarded, ignored, or destroyed inside an organization. LEGO is a prime example of a firm where that eco-system got out of balance and then subsequently restored, which helped the company rise to greatness again.

"By learning to build anything out of a simple material, children can combine right-brain creativity, storytelling and design thinking with left-brain scientific structure and logical analysis. For me that's where the soul of the company begins," says LEGO's executive chairman, Jørgen Vig Knudstorp.[89]

When Knudstorp joined LEGO in 2001, he found a company that had lost its soul. As Todd Weir explains in the *Marketing Journal*, LEGO "retired" many of its most successful and experienced engineers in the late 1990s, and then hired a new staff of "design experts" culled from the best colleges in Europe: "These folks knew little about toys, and even less about the practical application of plastic brick-work, let alone children at play. Under the new regime, the available LEGO parts quickly grew from 6,000 to over 12,000, creating a chaos of storage and logistics, and a huge growth of infrastructure, all of which brought little return on the sales floor."[90]

Knudstorp recruited hardcore LEGO fans known as AFOLs (Adult Fans of LEGO) to design products. LEGO also asked fans throughout the world to propose and then vote on possible new models and ideas. Knudstorp put the focus back on the core product, and he developed a product ethos to ensure that LEGO remained family friendly and true to its heritage, ensur-ing intergenerational knowledge and play. "What we realized is that the more we're true to ourselves, the better we are," he said. Thus, LEGO was reborn simply by returning to its origins of producing toys that make other toys.

For LEGO it was essential that people who loved the product became the designers of any new piece that saw the light of day. It sounds so

----

89　https://www.marketingjournal.org/a-toy-story-Lego-aristotle-and-business-of-play-todd-weir/

90　https://www.marketingjournal.org/a-toy-story-Lego-aristotle-and-business-of-play-todd-weir/

banal—but how often do we see companies fail in applying this key insight into their everyday work? Bringing their shared understanding and shared behaviors into balance *across everything they do* allows companies to be true to themselves and create corporate soul. Their ecosystem is intact.

This true self differs from company to company, but the principle remains universal since we are all human beings. Whether we work as an accountant, as an engineer, as a pilot, or as a chef—it's those principles of behavior that human beings have fostered over thousands of years. As Nigel Nicholson, business psychologist and professor at London Business School, stated in the *Harvard Business Review*:[91] "You can take the person out of the Stone Age, evolutionary psychologists contend, but you can't take the Stone Age out of the person. Human beings are, in other words, hardwired."

Identifying Ecosystem Elements and Creating Visibility on Progress

As workforces consist of vibrant and dynamic bodies of people, some stay in a company just for a year or two, while others are around for their lifetime. Thus, the essentials of the company ecosystem need to be reinforced—for the first group to understand where they have arrived and for the second group to contextualize how what mattered twenty years ago in one way has changed in the environment the company operates in today. Again, it is about creating a thoroughly shared understanding of what the Soul System™ is all about to allow the corresponding behaviors to happen across the enterprise.

Let's look at LEGO again. In an interview with BCG in 2017, Jørgen Vig Knudstorp explained what really matters at the company: "Our owners, being a family-controlled company, have always emphasized that we're here to serve the children. We're here to develop children. We're here to give children the very best. We want to be an irreplaceable but also

---

91   https://hbr.org/1998/07/how-hardwired-is-human-behavior

irresistible brand for children. We want to be on top of their wish list and something they talk passionately about."[92] For this, LEGO uses the Net Promoter Score, a metric that measures a business's customer experience and predicts growth. The company also measures how it creates value for customers and suppliers. "We really want to be sure that it is value creating for our customers and suppliers to work with us," Knudstorp said. On top of this, the company measures employees' engagement, which is the foundation of LEGO's reward system. According to Knudstorp, "We view financial value creation as the result of being highly recommended by children, highly value creating for our business partners, and having creative and engaged employees. If we have those three things, we cannot help but actually make a profit at the end of the day."

Amazing what level of clarity and simplicity that shows. Being on top of children's wish lists, as well as employee engagement and creating value for their business partners: It can be so simple.

Private Versus Public

Running a corporation via a "Management by Objectives" (MBO) approach has been common during the second half of the twentieth century, with companies like Hewlett-Packard adopting the approach and customizing it as the "HP Way."

Intel's Andy Grove leveraged MBO to arrive at his "Objectives and Key Results" (OKR) methodology—also known as iMBO (Intel's Management by Objectives). The following table from Whatmatters. com[93] illustrates the differences between the two concepts. In the context of the Soul System™, the public and transparent nature of the OKR methodology has significant advantages. It allows people to see the connection between shared understandings and desired shared behaviors

- - - - - - - - - - -

92   https://www.bcg.com/en-ch/publications/2017/people-organization-Jorgen-vig-knudstorp-Lego-growth-culture-not-kid-stuff

93   https://www.whatmatters.com/resources/okr-and-mbo-difference-between/

against the company's shared purpose. By using this methodology, enterprises can build a sound balance between the two and enable the company to build corporate soul.

MBOs	OKRs
"What"	"What" and "How"
Annual	Quarterly or Monthly
Private or Siloed	Public and Transparent
Top-Down	Bottom-Up or Sideways (-50%)
Tied to Compensation	Mostly Divorced from Compensation
Risk-Averse	Aggressive and Aspirational

Table 4: Comparison of MBOs versus OKRs.

Bruce Gil writes on Whatmatters.com, "OKRs aren't meant to encompass all of a company's work. They are not meant to track business-as-usual activities. According to John Doerr (author of *Measure What Matters*), they're supposed to track goals that 'merit special attention'—work that will get you closer to achieving your company's higher calling."[94] OKRs are a great tool to ensure alignment on all levels in order to bring shared purpose to life through shared understanding and shared behaviors. Culturestars editor Max Lamers wrote in a post on Medium[95] about high-performance cultures: "The whole reason of

> While it is quite an exercise to arrive at a compelling purpose statement plus the corresponding elements of shared understanding within the company, it is even harder to turn them into everyday reality.

----

94   https://www.whatmatters.com/faqs/okr-culture/

95   https://medium.com/culturestars/building-a-high-performance-culture-with-okrs-3407d3a94eb3

setting OKRs is to create purpose, alignment and focus on achieving goals that really move the business forward on all levels."

Easier Said Than Done

The Soul System™ starts with a shared purpose. While it is quite an exercise to arrive at a compelling purpose statement plus the corresponding elements of shared understanding within the company, it is even harder to turn them into everyday reality through shared behaviors. But the 2019 Business Roundtable statement (see chapter 1) has changed the dynamics significantly. The rising number of ESG investments across the world signals their impact: Global ESG assets are on track to exceed $53 trillion by 2025, representing more than a third of the $140.5 trillion in projected total assets under management.[96] Policy changes like the European Union's Green Deal or the United States pledging to cut carbon emissions by 50–52 percent below 2005 levels by the year 2030 are signaling significant change. Other key drivers are initiatives to fight inequality and foster diversity and inclusion. Everything adds up to a new level of change.

These external forces are pushing corporations to seriously consider and align everything they do to their purpose. But actually, it does not stop there. According to a Nielsen[97] study from 2018, "81% of global respondents feel strongly that companies should help improve the environment. This passion for corporate social responsibility is shared across gender lines and generations. Millennials, Gen Z, and Gen X are the most supportive, but their older counterparts aren't far behind."

While the pressure is mounting, the dynamics put leaders into a difficult position as they have to meet the new standards at the same time as

----

96   https://www.bloomberg.com/professional/blog/esg-assets-may-hit-53-trillion-by-2025-a-third-of-global-aum/

97   https://nielseniq.com/global/en/insights/analysis/2018/global-consumers-seek-companies-that-care-about-environmental-issues/

delivering results for their shareholders—and all of that in the context of a social media environment in which every mistake might become a topic for the public affairs department.

Companies have to take action on many levels.

The "low-hanging fruit" choices are the starting point to ensure stakeholders understand how current product lines and operational practices correspond to the company's shared purpose and shared understanding. In some areas, though, that won't be enough.

The "tough" choices require companies to provide sound explanations for both internal and external stakeholders to consent to difficult decisions that lead to significant changes to the way "things are done here."

The "hard" choices come into play when parts of the business no longer contribute to the purpose of the company. Closing or selling those divisions or areas of the business will only find acceptance if it is clearly linked to the purpose of the organization.

One of the most prominent examples of "hard" choices is CVS Health. Back in 2014, CVS Pharmacy became the first US drugstore chain to stop selling tobacco products. The company understood that tobacco didn't align with its purpose at the time of "helping people on their path to better health."[98] In line with its purpose, it offered a few programs to help smokers quit on top of removing tobacco products from its shelves. The results of this "hard" choice: $2 billion lost sales—but the other pharmacy sales jumped. In the eyes of the public, delivering on this "hard" choice allowed CVS Pharmacy to rebrand into CVS Health with huge credibility. Overall, a 10 percent increase in revenue occurred through the growth in pharmacy benefits management—a great example of how a shared purpose is the bedrock of a successful business.

- - - - - - - - - - -

98   https://cvshealth.com/about-cvs-health/our-purpose

A Long Way to Go

Management consultancy McKinsey & Company has provided a clear view on what it takes to deliver on a company's purpose in their "Embedding Purpose: Fewer Slogans, More Action" from August 2019. Their key point is this: "A corporate purpose is a commitment from the company to its stakeholders; its legitimacy derives from how the company embeds it and is seen to 'live' it. To that end, purpose should guide everything else and be evident in all a company does. A fully embedded purpose should show up across all elements of the organization's DNA."

The consultancy concludes that "while there are many inspiring examples of corporate choices being made, we would argue that no one (yet) has cracked the code of comprehensively embedding purpose across all elements of the company's DNA—although some companies are certainly far ahead of others. . . . We expect purpose will be one of the defining business issues of the next 20 years. Whether all stakeholders see companies embed it authentically will have a major effect on the future legitimacy of business in the eyes of society."

A fully embedded purpose should show up across 9 different elements of the organization's DNA

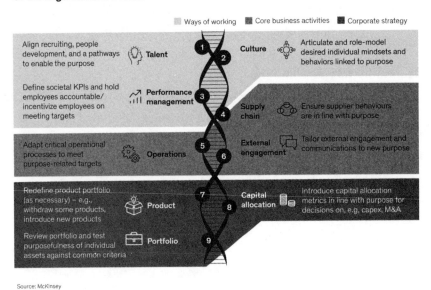

Source: McKinsey

Figure 11: McKinsey & Co. nine different elements of the organization's DNA.

Who Needs a Fur Coat?

For the luxury industry, social acceptance is everything. Nongovernmental organizations have been a constant pain in the neck to various categories, prompting boardroom and shareholder discussions about the social and environmental challenges businesses have to be prepared for. Everybody wants to avoid a situation where their category is proscribed by the public, such as the fur industry. By 2020, fur farming bans are in place in twenty countries.[99]

When it comes to luxury cars, the situation is very pointed. The Paris Agreement[100] set out a global framework to avoid dangerous climate change by limiting global warming to well below 2°C and pursuing efforts to limit it to 1.5°C. This framework has impacted the entire automotive industry, especially when it comes to SUVs and luxury cars, which have historically presented the most challenges when it comes to fuel consumption and emissions.

Today, the industry is in its largest transformation since Henry Ford invented the conveyor belt. A prime example of a company that has accepted the challenge is Bentley. As mentioned in chapter 4, the firm underwent a significant review of its strategic direction in 2018. CEO Adrian Hallmark and his leadership team turned every stone to make their site in Crewe, England, officially carbon neutral. They halved energy consumption and cut waste disposal by 98 percent. A 10,000 solar-panel car port supports the production site with renewable energy. But this is not enough to satisfy the ambition of management. Bentley aims to be fully ("end-to-end" as they call it) carbon neutral by 2030, and the Crewe factory is supposed to be climate positive after 2030.

By that time, all Bentley models will be fully electric, as the company transforms every aspect of its one-hundred-year-old business. Hallmark's "Beyond100" strategy announced in 2020 involves switching the entire model range to battery electric vehicles only. Evolving from the world's

----

99   https://www.furfreealliance.com/fur-bans/

100 https://ec.europa.eu/clima/policies/international/negotiations/paris_en

largest producer of 12-cylinder petrol engines to having no combustion engines within a decade will see Bentley reinvent itself as a world leader in sustainable luxury mobility.

As it moves into its second century, Bentley plans to become the world's most sustainable luxury carmaker. The shared purpose of Bentley has been the inspiration for that ambition: "To lead in sustainable luxury mobility." This is not just a pie-in-the-sky approach—84 percent of all Bentley cars ever built are still on the road. Sustainability is deeply rooted in the firm's DNA. This strategy is endorsed by the customers of the brand. Fifty-eight percent confirmed their purchase intention for an electric Bentley within the next five years. Walter Owen Bentley, who created the company with his simple and honest goal to build "a fast car, a good car, the best in class," would be proud of where the company is heading. "A good car" in today's day and age has to comply with environmental expectations that societies share the world over—especially in the luxury space. Otherwise, the fate of the fur coat is just around the corner.

How to Stay True to Purpose and Be Agile at the Same Time

One of the questions that is often raised is how to balance strategic consistency with tactical agility. In other words, how do you stay true to your company's shared purpose and be agile at the same time? Both are critical to make a company future-proof. One of the best real-life examples is Adobe. The company that is leading the Soul Index embraced integrity big time—and at the same time focused on excellence since the founding days. CEO Shantanu Narayen has been in the driver's seat since 2007.

Executive compensation consultant Seymour Burchman has taken a closer look at this important subject. His work focuses on reinforcing key strategies and leading to improved shareholder value through the identification of performance measures and goal-setting processes. In a 2020 article[101] in the *Harvard Business Review*, he takes a closer look at this issue.

- - - - - - - - - - -

101 https://hbr.org/2020/02/a-new-framework-for-executive-compensation

He summarizes by saying, "In the era of radical strategic transformation, executives and boards may have no choice but to consider how to make long-term incentives work better. If companies are to respond to disruptions, if they are to remain agile, if they are to rally stakeholders to work together to deliver outperformance in today's data-dependent business ecosystems, they risk getting behind the curve if they stick with standard incentive design today, which so prominently features three-year goal-setting processes based on financial measures." Burchman suggests that the framework of purpose, vision, and mission "can become 'true north,' not just as a driver of an extension of the past, but a springboard to the future."

What it requires, though, is a set of measures that are, according to Burchman, "enduring and not linked to the particulars of the strategy chosen for achieving them. In other words, they don't put a straitjacket on agile strategic changes during long-term transformation." Burchman looks at a hypothetical example with Southwest Airlines. "Dedication to the highest quality of customer service delivered with a sense of warmth, friendliness, individual pride, and company spirit." That is Southwest's mission to achieve its vision of becoming "the world's most loved, most flown, and most profitable airline," which is based on the airline's purpose: "Connect people to what's important in their lives through friendly, reliable, and low-cost air travel."

His analysis suggests that clear measurable performance goals such as the following would benefit not only Southwest's customers and employees but also shareholders significantly:[102]

- Customer measures, such as Net Promoter Score (loyalty), customer satisfaction score, and/or churn rate

- Employee engagement, attitudes, satisfaction, or turnover rates

- Number of passengers or passenger miles flown

- Brand strength relative to industry, over time

----

102 https://hbr.org/2020/02/a-new-framework-for-executive-compensation

- Returns relative to competitors, over time

- Profitability relative to competitors, over time

In his view, establishing "a bookend approach" would resolve any current disconnects: "Tying long-term incentives to the mission also allows a new, natural balance between annual and long-term incentives in influencing executive behavior. Short-term achievements can be rewarded in annual bonus plans and long-term outcomes in long-term plans."

Trade-Offs

Corporate life is driven by millions of decisions. Do you say yes to an idea, an initiative, an approach? Or do you dismiss it? The Soul System™ is actually a good compass for these moments of truth. Steve Jobs once made a strong connection in a comment he made about his own decision-making: "People think focus means saying yes to the thing you've got to focus on. But that's not what it means at all. It means saying no to the hundred other good ideas that there are. You have to pick carefully. I'm actually as proud of the things we haven't done as the things I have done. Innovation is saying no to 1,000 things."[103] Shared purpose is where the focus of the company starts. One company that is a perfect example for purpose-based focus—and the trade-offs that naturally result—is Patagonia.

> Corporate life is driven by millions of decisions. Do you say yes to an idea, an initiative, an approach? Or do you dismiss it? The Soul System™ is actually a good compass for these moments of truth.

Patagonia has been a special company from its start. Its founder Yvon Chouinard started the firm in 1973 as a rock-climbing outfitter that sold

---

103 https://www.forbes.com/sites/carminegallo/2011/05/16/steve-jobs-get-rid-of-the-crappy-stuff/

rugby shirts and corduroy shorts. Patagonia was never really supposed to do nearly a billion dollars in sales. Chouinard's Bauhaus-like design philosophy ensured that its products—like pile-fleece jackets, quick-dry shorts, and Pataloha Hawaiian shirts—soon became timeless outdoor icons. More than forty-five years later, the company has become synonymous with outdoor-minded pursuits. Its product offering also cannot be separated from its aggressive environmental advocacy. It leads the outdoor industry in using recycled nylon and polyester fabrics, and Patagonia's chilled-out vintage vibe is rooted in the idea that its clothes are built to last for years, not just seasons. Patagonia is a certified B Corp, a certification given to organizations that add value to employees and the environment (and not just shareholders). In September 2019, Patagonia was named a United Nations Champion of the Earth.[104]

Here comes the trade-off: On March 13, 2020, Patagonia shut down its physical *and* online businesses as a reaction to the COVID-19 pandemic. In a time where every retailer tried to rely on its online shops, that was a very surprising action. But it is fully plausible if you understand Patagonia. It has been at the cutting edge of social responsibility, environmental activism, and advocacy for public lands and the outdoors with a mission to "build the best product, cause no unnecessary harm, use business to inspire and implement solutions to the environmental crisis."[105] In view of the global climate change initiative, the founder and CEO of Patagonia changed its credo in 2018 to something much clearer: "Patagonia is in business to save our home planet." With that came a change in the company's directive to its Human Resources department: "Whenever we have a job opening, all things being equal, hire the person who's committed to saving the planet no matter what the job is." In the case of COVID-19, Patagonia's decision to pause online sales amid the pandemic came in part

- - - - - - - - - - - -

104   https://www.businessinsider.com/patagonia-un-champions-of-the-earth-award-2019

105   https://www.fastcompany.com/90280950/exclusive-patagonia-is-in-business-to-save-our-home-planet

out of management's concern for employees. Todd Soller,[106] head of global logistics and supply planning at Patagonia, said, "We knew we needed to take ample time to assess and design our new workplace procedures and layouts to address the threat of COVID-19." Five weeks later, the online service was reopened. New protocols were put into action—providing face masks and gloves to all on-site employees, temperature scans at all building entrances, staggered employee start times to avoid crowding, and frequent cleaning of surfaces—and business could begin again. Make no mistake, Patagonia not only took care of the health of its employees in the logistics center, but it also made sure that all employees would continue to receive their regular pay.

The soul ecosystem is probably the "sound equalizer" for the corporate soul. A little more bass? A bit less treble? More volume or less? Balancing the various aspects in a way that is true to a company's shared purpose and shared understanding is critical to ensuring consistently shared behaviors across that company.

---

106 https://www.forbes.com/sites/angelauyeung/2020/04/23/outdoor-clothing-chain-patagonia-yvon-chouinard-starts-selling-online-again-after-unusual-decision-to-pause-its-e-commerce-due-to-coronavirus-pandemic/?sh=373e571c1c48

Key thoughts to consider on
nurturing the soul ecosystem

	Soul Searching in Action
✓	Do your peers see the relationship between success and being true to the soul of the company?
✓	Have you identified what really matters and shared it with everyone?
✓	Have you gotten clear and simple KPIs at play?
✓	Are individual and collective activities managed through objectives and key results (OKR)?
✓	How seriously do you take ESG challenges? Do climate change, in-equality, and diversity and inclusion impact your short-, medium-, and long-term approach?
✓	Which societal KPIs are part of your corporate planning?
✓	How do you measure progress on the shared element of creating corporate soul?
✓	Are you prepared to accept short-term dips to secure the long-term health of your company and its soul?

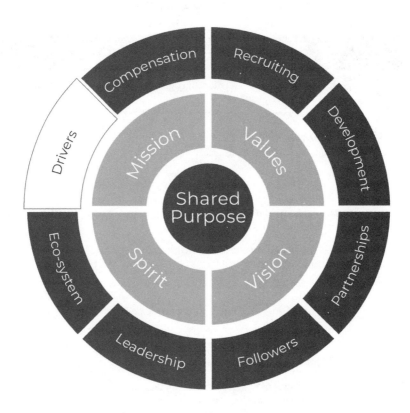

Figure 12: Soul drivers as a critical component within shared behaviors of the Soul System™.

CHAPTER 7

Promote Soul Drivers

How can you reward those within your organization
who are critical to the soul of your company at every level?

Chapter Goal:

Establish a mode of recognition for those who drive
corporate soul in your operation and provide them
with a transparent path for growth.

A t the height of Europe's migrant crisis in 2016, Robert Jung was working at EY in Germany. German chancellor Angela Merkel had become popular with some and not so popular with others when she made her famous assertion "Wir schaffen das" ("We can manage this"). She was convinced that Germany could manage to absorb very large numbers of immigrants. Jung was convinced, too, as was EY's managing director Ana-Cristina Grohnert. By chance, both of them watched a news program in which Syrian refugee and accountant by trade Mohammad Basel Alyounes was greeted by a German news crew.

When asked what he hoped for his new life in Germany, he responded, "I want to work for EY."[107]

Jung and Grohnert both took EY's purpose of "building a better working world" seriously, and it empowered them to take action. Within the following week Alyounes had joined EY through an internship program—and then his dream came true: He became a full-time employee at EY Germany. The story made its way through German media and obviously through the internal communication channels at EY. The firm concluded, "Colleagues around the world quickly heard the story and were captivated to learn how a mid-level EY manager was able to make this happen. Spreading Mohammad and Robert's story has inspired many professionals throughout EY's offices to live its purpose through a more socially conscious approach to making business decisions, from hiring new professionals to pursuing client services."[108]

This example illustrates several facets of the Soul System™: (1) The firm had a clear purpose and had created a shared understanding that went beyond the management team, (2) the firm's purpose and shared understanding transformed the shared behaviors of the firm's employees, and (3) the shared behaviors became a proof-point for everybody in the company to really believe that the purpose statement was not just a well-phrased declaration of intent, but also a real guiding principle for actions every day. The company's purpose is now loaded with authenticity and credibility, and that makes all the difference.

By the way, Robert Jung now heads up EY Germany's refugee support group. No surprise, Alyounes is a volunteer in this group. And both are probably better known in the company than many of the 270,000 employees—because the company's shared purpose now has a real-life story that is very human and people can easily relate to. They have served the purpose and its awareness in the company probably better than a

----

107 https://www.ey.com/en_us/purpose/how-can-society-gain-as-much-as-it-gives

108 https://www.ey.com/en_gl/purpose/is-your-purpose-lectured-or-lived

hundred townhall meetings of the executive team. Identifying *soul drivers* like Robert Jung is the key task for leaders in corporations to ensure that the soul of their company is strengthened. This is leading by example in the truest sense of the word.

What Makes It So Tough to Promote the Right Individuals?

Promotions are a very powerful tool—not only do they have the ability to increase employee morale beyond the individual who is being promoted, but they also are a credible sign to everyone else that career progression is possible internally. Plus, promoting individuals from within the organization who are ready for the next step often makes more sense than finding someone from the outside to both do the job and fit the culture of the company. Yet very often it is so much harder. In 2018, Michael C. Bush, CEO of Great Place to Work˚, and his colleagues Jessica Rohman and Chinwe Onyeagoro shared their experience based on a survey of over 400,000 US workers. The title says it all: "How You Promote People Can Make or Break Company Culture."[109]

> Employees are five times as likely to believe leaders act with integrity *if promotions have been managed in the right way.*

According to their history of thirty years of the Fortune 100 Best Companies to Work For ranking, employees are five times as likely to believe leaders act with integrity *if promotions have been managed in the right way.* For those being promoted, they claim that they are more than twice as likely to give extra effort at work and to plan a long-term future with their company. So, the benefits of getting it right are very straightforward. Not just for the people: "At these companies, stock returns are nearly three times the market average, voluntary turnover is half that of industry

- - - - - - - - - - -

109 https://hbr.org/2018/01/how-you-promote-people-can-make-or-break-company-culture

peers, and metrics for innovation, productivity, and growth consistently outperform competitors."

Why is it, then, that 25 percent of all employees in the 100 Best Companies that were researched believe promotions go to those who do not deserve them best? One can argue that 75 percent then believe these promotions are well deserved. But the authors state that within the overall study, that score of 75 percent "ranks as the third-lowest of all 58 items we assess."

Promotions are carefully watched by all the people impacted by them. Who is becoming my new team leader? Why did this person climb the corporate ladder—why not the colleague who is so much more friendly? Or—even worse—why did I not get the promotion? The impact promotions have is highly personal—and that means they are directly impacting the *perceived* culture of the firm. As we all know, perception is reality. Anything that is done in this area has the potential to be highly polarizing. If people perceive it as the right thing, the benefits are very positive. If not, the impact on morale of the workforce can be devastating. Again, it is these leadership behaviors that have the biggest impact on the corporate soul.

According to Lorena Martinez from Great Place to Work®,[110] not even half of all employees in the United States feel that a fair play is happening here. Lorena summarizes her decade of consulting experiences during which she has been in touch with many employees from many countries and industries: "I know that for the vast majority of them, the criteria for promotions are a mystery. Our research also indicates that fairness in promotions is most questioned when people do not have a chance to appeal the decision." She has developed eight core principles that leaders can use to create an environment that does not leave employees demotivated when it comes to promotions:

----

110   https://www.greatplacetowork.com/resources/blog/how-to-ensure-promotions-go-to-those-who-most-deserve-them

1. Care not only about employees' professional growth but also about their personal growth.

2. Give people the tools and opportunities to own and define their professional future, rather than deciding it for them.

3. Don't limit the growth of people by matching their background with the organizational chart.

4. Actively mentor people.

5. Create opportunities for exposure to senior leadership for everyone.

6. Encourage cross-department shadowing for people to develop new skills, and consider a career change in a new department.

7. Let people show their true selves.

8. Maximize human potential.

"Employees Practice the Behaviors That Are Valued, Not the Values Management Believes"

That quote[111] from Dr. Cameron Sepah continues: "Your company culture is who you hire, fire, and promote. The actual company values, as opposed to the nice-sounding values, are shown by who gets rewarded, promoted, or let go."

There is an old saying, "The fish stinks from its head down"—and it is true. It comes from the idea that when a fish rots, the first area to decompose is the head and then continues down the rest of the body. Head equals leadership. Failures in leadership work their way down the rest of the company. The bigger the failure, the faster the way down. Most of the time, these failures are small. That does not sound so problematic—but it actually is:

----

111 https://medium.com/s/company-culture/your-companys-culture-is-who-you-hire-fire-and-promote-c69f84902983

They are not so easy to detect. In companies that have created a shared understanding and shared behaviors around a clear and compelling purpose, such problems have a better chance to be identified. That's another reason why all elements of the Soul System™ have an impact on the way a business thrives. Sepah explains what he does to understand the reality in any given company: "Every time I walk into a new company I'm advising, I invariably encounter a set of noble values prominently displayed on the walls. The first thing I've trained myself to do is to not take them as gospel, and instead carefully observe how people *really* behave, which will tell me the actual values I need to know." He continues: "According to the theory of behaviorism, no behavior will persist long term unless it is being perpetuated by either a positive reinforcer (providing a reward, such as a promotion or praise) or a

> Shared behaviors make it much easier for every new employee to understand how the office "ticks" and allow them to adjust personal behaviors to those that the company wants to stand for.

negative reinforcer (removing a punishment, such as a probationary period or undesirable tasks). Thus, when companies start, leaders set the company's values not by what they write on the walls, but by how they actually act. For example, do they stay late and burn the midnight oil? Or do they leave early to be with their families?"

From my observations in many companies that I have had the pleasure to work with, I can only confirm his views. What he calls a "positive reinforcer" is what I call a *soul driver*. These people are priceless for any company since they are intrinsically supporting its shared behaviors.

A company is essentially a social environment—like families, like school classes, like sports teams. It is a combination of individuals against a common purpose—whether it is clearly stated or implicitly experienced. This is why a thorough understanding of the shared behaviors is so critical. These shared behaviors make it much easier for every new employee to understand how the office "ticks" and allow them to adjust personal behaviors to those that the company wants to stand for. The Wikipedia definition[112] of social learning theory provides a well-rounded understanding of what matters and why:

> Social learning theory is a theory of learning process and social behavior which proposes that new behaviors can be acquired by observing and imitating others. It states that learning is a cognitive process that takes place in a social context and can occur purely through observation or direct instruction, even in the absence of motor reproduction or direct reinforcement. In addition to the observation of behavior, learning also occurs through the observation of rewards and punishments, a process known as vicarious reinforcement. When a particular behavior is rewarded regularly, it will most likely persist; conversely, if a particular behavior is constantly punished, it will most likely desist. The theory expands on traditional behavioral theories, in which behavior is governed solely by reinforcements, by placing emphasis on the important roles of various internal processes in the learning individual.

Promotions are visible proof of what behaviors are valued—therefore a perfect opportunity to reinforce the corporate soul or to destroy it. Leaders determine the speed of the consequences of their actions, so they better do this consciously. In chapter 3, I explained the importance of purpose as the starting point and the importance of the founder generation. Start-ups ideally will grow, and in time, senior leadership may lose sight of what is happening on the ground. Sepah explains, "Employees begin to

> **Promotions are visible proof of what behaviors are valued—therefore a perfect opportunity to reinforce the corporate soul or to destroy it.**

----

112 https://en.wikipedia.org/wiki/Social_learning_theory

act according to what their managers either actively reinforce through praise and promotion or passively reinforce by allowance. Over time, employees become aware of which colleagues are being hired, fired, or promoted, and why."[113]

The Asshole Matrix

When it comes to promoting talent to the next level, you have *real* knowledge about an individual by that point. Identifying soul drivers for your company is critical if you want shared behaviors to endure as a means to ensure that the soul of your company is built to last. Sepah has developed a tool that details evaluating employees in a most straightforward way: the Asshole Matrix. But as the name of his tool indicates, it focuses on filtering out those who have a toxic impact on your company. Sepah provides a definition for the common-language term to avoid any misunderstandings: "Given that 'asshole' is not a clinical term, I will define it here as someone who lacks empathetic behavior to the point that it causes interpersonal issues."

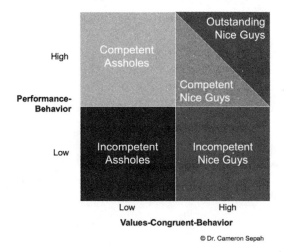

© Dr. Cameron Sepah

Figure 13: The Asshole Matrix by Dr. Cameron Sepah.

- - - - - - - - - - - -

113   https://medium.com/s/company-culture/your-companys-culture-is-who-you-hire-fire-and-promote-c69f84902983

He designed and helped implement this system of making values-congruent behavior a formal and prioritized part of the company's performance management process—pretty much the way we put values and behaviors into the focus of the evaluations that every employee was a part of three times a year (initially quarterly) at Spark44. His four-box matrix, though, makes an important leap as it does not stop with values and behaviors but adds the performance dimension to it:

INCOMPETENT ASSHOLES (FIRE FAST)

These are individuals you as a leader should really act fast on. Once you have come to the conclusion that their performance is low *and* their behavior does not comply, make up your mind and let them go. It is much better for the entire team if someone who operates in a toxic way does not continue to disturb a team that lives the shared behaviors. This person adds more work to the team through their incompetency. Sometimes, these are really hard decisions. You have pulled every string to hire someone you believe brings the competencies that the team lacked and would be a good fit, too. If this happens regularly, you should take a closer look at your approach to hiring.

COMPETENT ASSHOLES (REMEDIATE OR SEPARATE)

These folks create a very tough choice for every leader. Imagine that team member whose competencies are way above everybody else's—BUT (yes, it is a capital but) the way this person operates is so opposite to what the shared behaviors suggest that it can't be borne any longer. They are high performers, but in Sepah's words, "exhibit behavioral tendencies that are incongruent with company values." The choice you have is either tolerate (and thereby passively reinforce) that behavior and accept that everybody in the team or the entire company will start to believe that some guys can get away with everything. Or you follow Sepah's approach, which he calls "remediate or separate."

There's a reason Bob Sutton, a professor at the Stanford Graduate School of Business, developed the "No Asshole Rule." It's because exceptions shouldn't be made; otherwise it shows your values are merely aspirational.

Now, behaviors can change. In my experience, individuals when confronted often act surprised. They were simply not aware of their behaviors. That leaves a good chance to get them on what Sepah calls a "Values Improvement Plan." At our firm we chose three evaluations a year to ensure this could be managed—as a standard, we used 360-degree feedback (reviews from a direct supervisor, peers, and direct reports) once a year, but in cases where there were issues, we used this format for all three evaluations to monitor progress. But there are cases where it doesn't work. You have to be prepared to take final actions then. It all depends on the willingness of the individual to embrace the feedback—the person actually does their own soul searching. Every now and then it is worth involving a coach to help them get there, as I have seen it pay off more than once.

INCOMPETENT NICE GUYS (MANAGE OR MOVE)

These are tricky, too. You know them immediately when you read this; they exist in every organization: great people, very nice, but can't get anything done. Perhaps it is not "anything" but certain tasks that require a bit more effort. Sepah has a clear view: "Giving free license to someone to underperform just because they are kind or likeable sends the message that your company is not a meritocracy, and that it's more important to be socially skilled (or at worst, be a brown noser)." Your responsibility as a leader—remember, you made the decision to bring the person in—is to help them with their performance and provide training and feedback to get them there. Sometimes that does not do the trick. Then the question is on the table: Move them to a different role (I have seen that do wonders) or move them out.

COMPETENT AND OUTSTANDING NICE GUYS
(PRAISE AND RAISE)

At Spark44, we called these people rock stars. As the CEO, I made sure that they knew why we thought they were rock stars—and leveraged their combination of performance and behavior to demonstrate them as role models inside the organization. Whether it was about their move to the next phase of their career or international moves, these rock stars were the backbone of our organization. They are what Sarah Tavel of the venture capital firm Greylock Partners calls the "mitochondria in start-ups, because they are the company's power plants—adding value beyond their job description by asking and doing what is best for the company."[114]

The Theory Is Compelling— What Do You Do?

When we promote individuals, we need to be mindful of the factor of the relationship we have with the individual when we make the call. As the Asshole Matrix suggests, the relationship (e.g., nice guy) is only one part of the equation. It is important to ensure that the process of promoting individuals is transparent and considered fair by all. It actually starts way before any promotion is considered. A leader at every level must understand the aspirations that are at play:

- What is it that the team members want to become?
- Do they know what their potential is?
- Are they aware of how they are being perceived by colleagues?

At Spark44, our evaluation process focused on values and performance. It was linked to a bonus payment depending on the score that was achieved. Each of these evaluation meetings offered an opportunity for both the leader

----

114 https://sarahtavel.medium.com/the-mitochondria-in-startups-dc6c33e09d99

and the associate to mirror their perceptions and consider the reality both had of each other. While at one of these quarterly sessions, a "what does your mid-term or long-term future look like" conversation was mandatory; in many cases these discussions happened regularly whenever one of the two saw the need. For the manager it was an opportunity to identify how they could support the individual in the area where it was needed—and to agree to next steps to ensure things were moving in the right direction. It contained an understanding about where the gaps were so that, via training or mentoring, individuals could close them organically. It was a highly powerful tool.

When it worked at its full potential, it was great to see managers sharing with their leaders who the high-potential employees were. We used a nine-box grid to manage the different stages of performance and potential in the role the individual was operating in. This created a platform for a discussion—which actually was as important as the findings—between manager and employee to ensure that both had a shared view of the state of the union.

	Low	Performance	High
High	**Developer** *12 month development plan to stretch in current role. Focus on core job skills*	**Emerging Star** *6-12 month development plan to bridge next level*	**Rock Star** *Accelerated career progression*
Potential	**Learner** *Stretch in current role through regular feedback and clear direction*	**Solid Contributor** *Stretch skills, confidence and risk taking in current role*	**Emerging Star** *6-12 month development plan to bridge next level*
Low	**Actionable** *Poor hire/wrong role? Manage performance*	**Contributor** *Provide clear direction and build confidence*	**Reliable Professional** *Build commitment and motivation. Stretch scope of current role*

Figure 14: Nine-box evaluation grid.

There is not a single process that is perfect. We felt the logic of the nine-box approach was compelling. It worked well on an individual office level—but when we compared offices, it became obvious that there were a few pitfalls that we had to be aware of. Some were driven by individual biases, some by cultural nuances around the world—some cultures find it easier than others to express truths. As with all processes, get started and improve on the way.

What Promotion Opportunities Exist?

One of the most common complaints about promotion opportunities is that people feel that they are not aware of them when it is relevant. There are many Glassdoor mentions where employees complain that the decision about the potential candidate is a fait accompli—in other words, when they learn about the opportunity, the decision has already been made. Obviously, this is a killer when it comes to employee engagement. They feel they have no chance.

For leaders, that means that they have to be transparent in openings that are coming up. They actually have a perfect opportunity to share the good news—the fact the company grows any new openings is a chance to ensure employees recognize that the firm's success provides real opportunities to them. In the case of replacing an existing position, it is a sign of the confidence that leaders put into their associates to have the caliber to step up. This trust is one of the key behaviors that associates want from their leaders. At Spark44 I used every chance to offer opportunities at the central offices to hire potential employees from other locations outside the United Kingdom. To ensure the shared purpose of the company was well spread across the globe, I pushed hard at every opportunity to transfer those who were dyed in the wool with corporate soul to other places and lead people to achieve what they did not believe possible. This notion was a common theme of the thank-you messages that I received from colleagues around the world when my departure was communicated.

Encouraging individuals to actually understand their potential—even if they don't see it yet—is one of the most fulfilling leadership opportunities. Seeing people thrive is simply great.

Managing the News

Every leader knows this situation: A promotion opportunity exists. One person gets the promotion, while the other applicants don't. This calls for active communication about why that particular decision was made. It is not about "she ticked more boxes in the job description than anyone else;" it is about contextualizing the decision with the other candidates. As a *Harvard Business Review* article about promotion[115] outlines—and in my own experience—it is one of those situations that is often not managed well: "Once the decision is made: generate buy-in. Everyone is curious to learn the 'who' component of a promotion decision. However, the opportunity to fully engage people lies in explaining *why* the decision was made. Rather than rehash criteria from the job description, share inspiring stories and examples of how the individual consistently met the criteria, and also, how their promotion benefits the broader team."

Both with my own hires and with hires from my direct reports, I have seen this happen. It is tough—very often when these decisions are made, the "distance" between the one who gets the promotion and the one who doesn't feels more like the distance between the gold medal winner and the silver medalist at a hundred-meter final, rather than the minutes between first and second at a marathon. Explaining to individuals why they did not make it is critical, but be prepared that from their point of view, the split-second difference would have been in their favor. The way out that the *Harvard Business Review* article suggests is definitely worth a try: "'Every time I promote one person, I disappoint 10 others,' [a business leader] lamented. His colleague, who led the company's research division, said

----

115 https://hbr.org/2018/01/how-you-promote-people-can-make-or-break-company-culture

he too was challenged in this way. To address the dynamic, he partners with his leaders as a group to discuss how the organization's growth goals will create opportunities for each team member to grow and advance over time." This approach allows for a shared sense of ownership that can make a real difference in the short- and long-term.

Consider that most employees work hard to achieve a promotion. The news that they have been successful in getting the new position is definitely a reason to celebrate—but for leaders it is critical that they manage this moment with sophistication. One key element is to obviously share the news in a one-on-one conversation and confirm it with a formal promotion letter. This is key—often misunderstandings occur at this moment. The letter provides a written record of what the promotion involves, what is expected from the employee in their new role, and the qualities, skills, and achievements that led to the promotion. Another key element is to look at the promotion announcement as an opportunity to reinforce the characteristics of a soul driver to ensure the entire organization understands the importance that corporate soul has for the firm. It might be just an additional sentence, but people will remember it since it moves the announcement from a purely rational one to a more balanced—perhaps even empathetic—approach. I always encouraged my team to include a line on what made the person a rock star and why that created the opportunity for the next move. People get it.

Depending on the size of the organization, announcements are often handled via an all-staff email. HR professionals recommend outlining the reasons for the promotion, keeping the tone professional, and asking coworkers to join you in congratulating their newly promoted colleague. Again, depending on the size and location structure, this announcement can be done in a regular team meeting—either in person or via a web conference call. It is critical to clearly explain the responsibilities of the role and what changes there will be, and to ask the team to be open about any questions. It is not unusual that in these sessions people do not speak up. Therefore, it is important to allow for time to check in with the colleagues and give them space for raising any issues and concerns in a one-on-one setting.

It goes without saying that when the promotion is of public interest, any press announcements come in second. "Ohana means family" is the Salesforce mantra.[116] And important things are better discussed inside the family before they are shared with others. Anybody who has ever learned that they were not considered in a promotion situation through the press agrees that this can seriously hurt.

After the Game Is Before the (Next) Game

Germany's former national football (soccer for my US readers) team coach Sepp Herberger, who led the squad winning the 1954 World Championship, shaped this saying, which informed his approach to sports: There is always another opportunity to focus on. The same is true for those who did not get the promotion—although they might have thought that they "deserved" it more. The Great Place to Work® team[117] calls this the moment of recalibration: "Was the issue a matter of readiness ('not now'), aspiration ('not this'), or an issue with the company overall ('not here')? In all cases, your support at this juncture is critical to that person's future success." Similar to the findings from the Asshole Matrix, it is a question of finding the right people for any given task. Sometimes you have the right people, but for very different tasks. Using those moments to do justice to the adage "Sometimes you win, sometimes you learn" is actually priceless. I have personally seen it more than once: Systematically empowering leaders at every level to use these principles within their teams creates tangible results. The Great Place to Work® team echoes my experiences: "These will be remarkable as more people across the company re-connect with their aspirations, feel a sense of sponsorship, extend trust to leaders when

----

116 https://www.salesforceben.com/what-is-the-salesforce-ohana/

117 https://hbr.org/2018/01/how-you-promote-people-can-make-or-break-company-culture

promotion decisions are made, and get excited about what's possible as a valued member of a winning team."

Don't Miss Out on the Hidden Soul Drivers

Sometimes, these soul drivers are hidden in your organization. But you can only promote those of whom you are aware—very banal, but true. Pamela DeLoatch is a B2B technology writer specializing in creating marketing content for the HR industry. With a background as an HR generalist and specialist, she writes about the employee experience, engagement, diversity, HR leadership, culture, and technology. In one of her blogs,[118] she points at one of the areas that is often overlooked: "Not all qualified candidates are equally considered for promotions." For her, there are two large groups of underrepresented candidates:

- those without a champion, or

- those without similarities to leaders (race, gender, language, school, sports, family, etc.)

Often, they are being overlooked. Pamela DeLoatch: "This can easily happen, especially when you consider this: women apply for positions if they meet 100% of the criteria, while men apply if they only meet 60%."

I have seen this too—"apparently," person X was *the only choice*. Especially in a global organization, sometimes the *only* choice somewhere is not the only choice everywhere. Creating an environment where people are encouraged to apply for jobs in a foreign country if they feel it would be their next great step in their career is one thing—making managers support that approach is a different kettle of fish. Asking managers to look at the greater good of the organization is something many have to get used to. Very often, my final convincing argument was this:

----

118 https://www.15five.com/blog/employee-promotion-strategy-work-culture/

Person X is on the move, so if we don't provide an opportunity, they will be gone to a different company. Then you as the manager lose them and we as a company do, too.

Pamela DeLoatch recommends being intentional in seeking out and considering all qualified candidates and cites an example from the sports category: "In order to increase diversity in coaching and management, the NFL requires teams to interview minority candidates for head coaching and general manager positions [the Rooney Rule]. Although your efforts don't have to be solely about race, use the Rooney Rule for inspiration: look for those invisible candidates, ones you don't know as well or have as much in common with. Yes, you still want to find the best candidates for promotion—but you might not if you prematurely limit your pool of possibilities. By widening your lens your actions reflect that everyone's contributions are important, that the promotion process is fair, and that you are committed to diversity and inclusion."

Great Managers Are a Rare Species

One of the biggest issues is identifying individuals who are capable of being a great manager. In 2015, Gallup—known as one of the world's leading research firms, as well as a global analytics and advice firm that helps leaders and organizations solve their most pressing problems—issued the report "State of the American Manager: Analytics and Advice for Leaders."[119] It showed that in eight out of ten cases, promoting an employee into a job that needs skills they don't have does not work out.

Leadership consultant and author (*Lead from the Heart*) Mark C. Crowley identified five key findings from the Gallup study:[120]

1. The majority of managers are wrong for their roles.

- - - - - - - - - - -

119 https://www.gallup.com/services/182138/state-american-manager.aspx

120 https://www.fastcompany.com/3045453/how-the-wrong-people-get-promoted-and-how-to-change-it

2. Great managers possess a rare combination of five talents.

3. Managers have the greatest impact on engagement.

4. Female managers are much more effective at driving engagement.

5. High talent managers focus on strengths, not on weaknesses.

These five points help companies stay focused on valuing and pro-moting soul drivers when it comes to selecting people into management. Being great in one area of the business is not necessarily the perfect quali-fication to move into a management position. I have seen too many people who were great in their profession but failed when they felt the burden of responsibility on their shoulders. As leaders, though, we know that making the right decision when it comes to promoting a leader is critical to the success of any team—or even critical to the future of the entire company.

"It is the rite of passage in most organizations that if you are very good at your job—whether it be in sales, or accounting, or any number of specialties—and stay around a long time, the next step in your pro-gression is to be promoted to manager," says Jim Harter, Gallup's chief scientist. "But the talents that make a person successful in a previous, non-management role are almost never the same ones that will make them excel as a manager."

The Gallup study states pay structures at most companies reinforce this career progression and must be redesigned to ensure employees are given more than one path to earning higher compensation and prestige. According to the report, organizations back themselves into a corner when they tie pay to managerial status, creating an environment in which employees compete for roles to which they're not a fit.

By the way, what Jim Harter describes is also known as the Peter Principle. Wikipedia describes it as follows:[121]

- - - - - - - - - - -

121 https://en.wikipedia.org/wiki/Peter_principle

The Peter Principle is a concept in management developed by Laurence J. Peter, which observes that people in a hierarchy tend to rise to their "level of incompetence": employees are promoted based on their success in previous jobs until they reach a level at which they are no longer competent, as skills in one job do not necessarily translate to another. The concept was explained in the 1969 book *The Peter Principle* by Dr. Peter and Raymond Hull. [The authors] intended the book to be satire, but it became popular as it was seen to make a serious point about the shortcomings of how people are promoted within hierarchical organizations. Hull wrote the text, based on Peter's research. The Peter Principle has been the subject of much subsequent commentary and research.

Gallup studied individual managers at numerous organizations and discovered those managers who most consistently drove high engagement, loyalty, productivity, profit, and service levels all shared five uncommon talents:[122]

1. They motivate their employees.

2. They assert themselves to overcome obstacles.

3. They create a culture of accountability.

4. They build trusting relationships.

5. They make informed, unbiased decisions for the good of their team and organization.

Gallup confirmed that this combination of innate talent is so rare that it exists in about only one out of ten people. They also believe another two

----

122 https://www.fastcompany.com/3045453/how-the-wrong-people-get-promoted-and-how-to-change-it

out of ten people have some of these five talents and can become great managers with the right coaching and development.

Ironically, Harter is convinced that the most highly talented manager prospects are hiding in plain sight within organizations, and the use of some predictive analytics tools can help companies make more informed hiring decisions. The rewards for doing so are impressive. Companies already employing the predictive analytics tools have realized a 48 percent increase in profitability, a 22 percent increase in productivity, and a 30 percent jump in engagement scores, the Gallup report notes.

Another stunning finding in Gallup's study is that employees of female managers on average are at least 6 percentage points more engaged than those who work for a male manager. In fact, out of the twelve questions Gallup uses to diagnose a person's engagement, employees of female managers outscore male managers on eleven of them.

Only one out of three workers have a female boss today, yet women leaders eclipse their male counterparts in many of the ways known to inspire high levels of commitment, initiative, and loyalty in twenty-first-century workers. They more consistently cultivate the potential in their people by creating challenging assignments. They praise and value people for their efforts and contributions. They take steps to foster a positive and cooperative work environment.

In their 2013 book, *The Athena Doctrine: How Women (and the Men Who Think Like Them) Will Rule the Future*, authors Michael D'Antonio and John Gerzema note that the skills required to thrive in today's world—such as honesty, empathy, communication, appreciation, and collaboration—are widely regarded as being on the feminine side of human nature. Gallup's data suggests many of these same qualities have a significant and meaningful impact on driving engagement.

Gallup has studied engagement since the 1990s and has repeatedly found that companies with happy and committed employees outperform all others in terms of business outcomes, including absenteeism, turnover, innovation, and productivity. Accentuating positive behaviors and traits in people has proven to be a wildly more successful approach to driving engagement than a well-intended focus on mitigating weakness, Gallup says. In their study of more than a thousand random US workers, nearly two-thirds, or 61 percent, of employees who felt they had a manager who honored and intentionally amplified their positive characteristics were engaged—twice the national average.

Overall, Gallup has discovered that the managers—regardless of gender—who routinely motivate the greatest employee engagement have an instinct for investing emotionally in their people. Workers describe them as being more human and relatable—someone who cares about them personally and with whom they can discuss nonwork-related issues.

These same high-talent managers also make communication a priority. They hold regular meetings and interact with each employee in some way every single day. Simply put, they make their people feel valued and connected, which has the direct effect of sending engagement soaring.

The findings of the Gallup study relate to the United States, but it is probably fair to say that the tendency is pretty universal. Given the amount that companies spend on leadership training, it's a disturbing finding that, in most cases, people who are promoted into a position for which they don't have the skills don't succeed.

Soul drivers are a rare species—identifying them is really critical when you are on your way to building a company with soul. Once your organization has been able to find them, make sure they are being nurtured and given the opportunities to grow. They are definitely worth it.

Key thoughts to consider on promoting soul drivers

	Soul Searching in Action
✓	How many soul drivers did you recognize this past month, quarter, or year?
✓	Are your leaders able to transform challenging practices by employees into actions to protect and incentivize the values management believes in?
✓	Do you regularly identify individuals who support or oppose your company's shared understanding through their behaviors?
✓	Do you have a proactive approach in place to ensure soul drivers are aware of promotion opportunities?
✓	Are you engaging proactively with peers who are not considered for a promotion to explain why they have not been considered?
✓	Have you ensured that potential soul drivers are being mentored and championed in the organization?
✓	How do you identify great future managers—which criteria are you evaluating?
✓	Do you review employee engagement scores with a view to the quality of their managers?

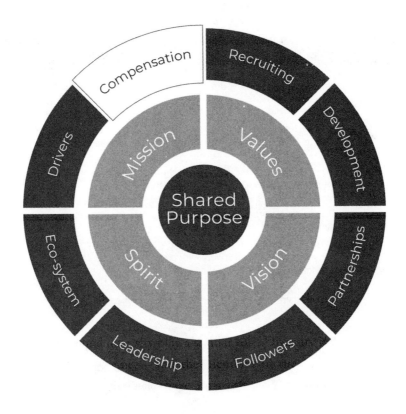

Figure 15: Fair compensation of soul supporters as a
critical element of the shared behaviors of the Soul System™.

CHAPTER 8

Reward Soul Supporters

How can you identify the key members of the backstage crew who are allowing the frontline staff to perform and represent the company at its best?

Chapter Goal:

Understand the importance of staff members at all levels and the tools to ensure that compensation and evaluation mechanisms are supporting your corporate soul.

W hen you read about corporate culture, the CEO or managing director is usually the person in the spotlight. One thing is true: Without a committed CEO or managing director, corporate soul can be difficult to emerge. But corporate soul needs more than just a strong leader.

It's a bit like a rock 'n' roll concert: The band performs and the entire focus is rightly on them. However, without the roadies, the lighting technicians, the sound engineers, the caterers, and many more support staff, that performance would simply not happen. These roles are critical to building rock 'n' roll soul. In corporations it is the same. An example of a housekeeper at a German automotive company impressed me big-time: At a press event he noticed that a bar table did not stand firmly on the ground, but moved to either side when anyone leaned on it. He took his screwdriver and drilled a few screws into the legs of the table. The journalists at the table were surprised and asked him why he did it. His answer: "This company is all about precision. We fix things when we notice them." He did what he believed was right based on the shared understanding and the shared behaviors of the company. The journalist was so impressed that he had to write about it. That night, he met a true soul supporter.

That housekeeper was obviously not a member of the executive team and definitely not one of the most highly paid individuals in the firm. And that is true for millions of people in many jobs—so it is critical that corporations view their compensation packages in the light of their corporate soul. How can companies ensure that their salary and incentive packages are not just competitive, but also in line with the purpose of the company and the values that it does claim to be driven by? The Salesforce example highlighted in chapter 5 showed how to synchronize the value of equality with compensation structure.

The 2017 EY study "How Can Purpose Reveal a Path through Disruption?"[123] shows that 37 percent of employees think their performance isn't linked to their organization's purpose—with a similar share of employees stating that salaries and remuneration incentives are not connected to the purpose of their employer. If you look at this with a "glass half full" view, then you can be confident in saying more than half of all companies have aligned their compensation packages to their purpose. In other words, their behavior is a shared behavior aligned with

----

123   https://assets.ey.com/content/dam/ey-sites/ey-com/en_gl/topics/purpose/purpose-pdfs/ey-how-can-purpose-reveal-a-path-through-uncertainty.pdf

their shared understanding of vision, mission, values, and spirit. But if you just take stock of these percentages, it becomes obvious that there is a lot to be done.

The study concludes, "If purpose really matters, it will be incorporated into the performance metrics of individual employees, from job descriptions to KPIs to compensation." Bonus schemes that measure achievements against goals that are inextricably linked to the corporation's purpose are one way to do it. EY quotes a global materials and life sciences company that puts sustainability at the heart of its purpose. This company bases 50 percent of senior executives' short-term bonuses on how effectively the firm meets their sustainability goals. By doing it this way they definitely accelerate their path to sustainability—and at the same time ensure that everybody in the company does not miss the key element of their purpose.

It is very interesting that if you Google "purpose-based compensation structure" that you really don't find any immediate hits. The first relevant mention is Glassdoor's "The Benefits and Compensation Models of the Future"[124]

> In the language of the Soul System™, "beliefs" are synonymous with values.

white paper. Their chief economist Andrew Chamberlain predicts "a new wave of culture-first thinking among business leaders, elevating employee engagement to the status of core business focus for a growing number of companies."[125]

That's what best-in-class, purposeful companies already do. EY research[126] found that more than 90 percent of them regularly evaluate whether they're making progress toward their purpose. They align

----

124 https://www.glassdoor.com/employers/blog/compensation-benefits-models-future/

125 https://www.glassdoor.com/employers/blog/why-businesses-are-becoming-more-employee-centric-in-2020/

126 https://www.ey.com/en_gl/purpose/is-your-purpose-lectured-or-lived

purpose and performance metrics at an organization-wide level. The report says as follows:

> These metrics aren't just measured in dollars. Sometimes, the most effective way to tell whether a company is living its purpose is employee feedback. Other firms might find surveys of employee well-being or net-promoter scores to be more effective metrics. The specific tactics are less important than the broader point: organizations need to build a means of tracking progress on their purpose journey. And executives have to be brave enough to ask for honest input from their employees and have the courage to really listen and act decisively on what they hear. One multinational diversified industrial firm polls its employees on a regular basis "to make sure that the beliefs of the organization are being seen" by them. One of the firm's leaders told us, "it's sometimes said that culture of purpose statement is 'touchy feely.'" But truly making purpose stick requires both qualitative and quantitative metrics.

In the language of the Soul System™, "beliefs" are synonymous with values.

Compensation beyond the Paycheck

Rent is the highest monthly cost factor most employees need to consider. Even if the salary package is good, this is a big issue all over the world. San Francisco, New York, London, Dublin, Zurich, Munich, Singapore, Shanghai, and Tokyo—the list goes on and on. Some companies have gone back to offering corporate housing, a practice that was common decades ago. LEGO is offering small apartments for workers as part of its new global headquarters. IKEA is approaching the issue with an apartment building in Reykjavik (Iceland), and Samsung runs a cluster of apartment buildings in Seoul and Suwon, South Korea. When I started my professional career, the apartments that my first employer Bertelsmann rented out were a great help. Going back even further is the Fuggerei in Augsburg, Germany, one of the world's oldest social housing complexes still in use.[127] The name stems from the Fugger family who created the place in 1516 where Augsburg citizens in need could find housing. Within seven years the area grew to fifty-two houses with further streets and even a church being added to the Fuggerei. It was actually a gated community; to a certain degree, one could compare it to a small independent town in the medieval age.

Today, instead of investing in brick and mortar, some Chinese companies are offering support in a different way: With Tencent, the Chinese multinational tech conglomerate that offers various internet-related services and products, interest-free loans are offered to help employees buy real estate in the city. Starbucks offers its full-time workers in China financial support to cover part of their rent.[128]

Across All Ranks

A case study on hotel giant Hilton by Great Place to Work® indicates that the largest gaps that exist in the workplace experience among different demographic groups are between employees in different job levels. The rule of thumb across any organization is that the higher you are in the organization, the better the work experience tends to be—the corner office and all the different perks that come with it. The key differences between frontline employees and leaders tend to be in the areas of fairness, communication, and meaningful work. For example, individual contributors are far less likely than executives to believe that they are involved in decisions that affect their job or work environment, or that managers genuinely seek

- - - - - - - - - - -

127 https://en.wikipedia.org/wiki/Fuggerei

128 https://www.seattletimes.com/business/retail/starbucks-to-help-pay-for-china-
     workers-housing/

and respond to their suggestions and ideas. The Great Place to Work* study finds that "employees who are not in management or leadership roles are more likely to feel like a replaceable 'cog in the wheel' rather than a valued member of the team. It's tough to show care for a guest or a customer when you're feeling like a cog yourself."[129]

Hilton CEO Chris Nassetta revolutionized that paradigm—not in a twenty-person office environment somewhere but in a global business of hundreds of thousands of people across all continents.

Under Nassetta's leadership, Hilton made a commitment to treat all staff members as well as it treats the guests at all of its hotels. He reinforced one point over and over again—to drive a culture that values the contribution of every member of the staff. That effort has paid off, according to the Great Place to Work* study. It reported that between 2012 and 2017, Hilton showed an increase in the trust level that the lower to mid-level ranks have in the company (see figure 16). Frontline managers, as well as the C-suite, gained 5 percentage points over this period. The trust of "individual contributors," or the people ranked below manager status, increased by 11 percentage points.

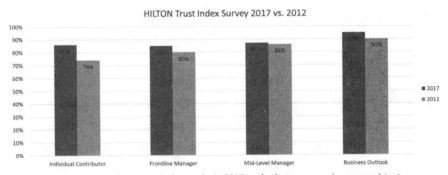

Average employee trust index results in 2017 are both stronger and more consistent.

Source: Great Place to Work

Figure 16: Great Place to Work® Hilton Trust survey, 2017 vs. 2012.

- - - - - - - - - - - -

129 https://www.greatplacetowork.com/images/reports/2018-GPTW-Profile-Series-_Hilton_Hospitality_For_All.pdf

The efforts that Hilton put into the relaunch of the brand, the extension of the portfolio, the digitization actions, and the customer loyalty program would have not worked out that extensively if the global staff had not been seriously allowed to participate in that journey. One of Nassetta's key objectives was to improve benefits across the company's wide spectrum of employees, from housekeepers to HR managers. In 2018, Hilton extended its parental leave policy, guaranteeing twelve weeks of paid time off for new mothers, and four for fathers and adoptive parents. The company also partnered with the start-up Milk Stork, enabling team members to easily ship or carry breast milk when traveling for work, for free. The company continued its rollout of an employee stock purchase program— at all levels of the company, regardless of position. And Hilton employees continue to enjoy a travel program that allows team members to become customers themselves at locations around the world at highly discounted rates. (For more about Hilton's employee programs, see the case study in the appendix and check www.greatplacetowork.com.)

A Path to Success

The Great Place to Work° case study shares as well how Hilton describes its progress in recent years in sequential terms:[130]

1. Start with a clear set of values and a sense of purpose.

2. Design core programs aligned to those values.

3. Hold leaders accountable for living the values and breathing life into the programs.

4. Put programs in place and strive to make high performance sustainable.

---

130 https://www.greatplacetowork.com/images/reports/2018-GPTW-Profile-Series-_Hilton_ Hospitality_For_All.pdf

5. Invest in frontline team members, with higher engagement and retention delivering a return on that investment.

6. Measure performance and employee experience, using data to refine and improve.

The case study also includes a key backstage example that illustrates Hilton's commitment to its employees: the renovated housekeeping staff room at the Hilton San Francisco Union Square. According to Christine Himpler, the director of housekeeping, the new staff lounge changed the way she interacts with her team. The formerly sterile room is now warm and inviting, with three couches where employees feel more at ease and more valued. When Himpler has to talk with staff about problems, the conversations don't feel like strict disciplinary proceedings, which has allowed her to build her team's camaraderie and solidarity.

Chris Nassetta has been able to build corporate soul by creating shared behaviors built upon a shared understanding of the company's vision, mission, values, and spirit.

Recognizing Cultural Humility, Privilege, and Bias

Whether your company is an international enterprise or a domestic business, there aren't many corporations these days where every member of the workforce stems from the same gender or ethnicity. In other words, don't expect that everyone else has the same perspective on what is going on at your firm. To state the obvious, soul supporters can come from anywhere with any kind of background or orientation. Often, though, leaders in corporations do not look at it this way. One positive example here is LinkedIn, where Nuhamin Woldemariam, a global program manager on the Diversity, Inclusion, and Belonging (DIBs) team, developed a globally focused Allyship Academy that's now in fourteen countries. "We need to talk about things like bias, cultural humility, power and privilege, and broadening our views," she said. "A lot of my work is about developing managers to be inclusive leaders."[131] The keyword here is *developing*. This is not a "say it once, and everything will change" approach. The academy creates Allyship Ambassadors who are then building a movement within each of their LinkedIn offices, curating powerful peer-led conversations on the importance of allyship behaviors, identifying bias in the workplace, and role-modeling courageous conversations in their organizations.

Humility equals the state of being humble. But what is it that defines humble leadership? Definitely not "low" (which would be the straight translation of the Latin word humilis). I would rather translate it as *self-reflected leadership*. That means understanding the strengths others bring to the table and a real openness to feedback and ideas that they offer. Make no mistake: Being humble does not exclude being driven or ambitious.

In their 2019 article "How to infuse your company culture with humility," [132] Dusya Vera, Ph.D., who is a professor of strategic management at the C. T. Bauer College of Business at the University of Houston and Tiffany Maldonado, Ph.D., who is a visiting assistant professor in the Marilyn Davies College of Business at the University of Houston-Downtown identified six norms to improve organizational culture with a sense of humility. The six norms help workplaces embrace the generosity, cohesion, and learning that lead to success:

- Accurate awareness
- Tolerating competent mistakes
- Transparency and honesty
- Openness
- Employee development
- Employee recognition

- - - - - - - - - - - -

131 https://blogs.haas.berkeley.edu/the-berkeley-mba/a-focus-on-diversity-equity-and-inclusion-and-allyship-drives-this-berkeley-mba

132 https://greatergood.berkeley.edu/article/item/how_to_infuse_your_company_culture_with_humility

Just reading these bullet points should make your imagination paint a picture of an organization with soul. Accurate awareness means ensuring a shared understanding by all about vision, mission, values, and spirit. And tolerating competent mistakes provides space for taking considered risks inside a company, which is critical when it comes to innovation. Transparency and honesty are what I call the "anti-silo" drug. Organizations gain so much when their people can talk openly about what's going on and individuals can build on ideas from others and make them stronger. The same goes for openness—the opposite of "not invented here." Like the Allyship Academy, employee development is a priority for humble organizations. Last, but not least, recognizing and celebrating the successes of their people is a real sign of a humble organization.

The extreme increase in LinkedIn users over the years has fueled this growth. When the Microsoft acquisition happened, the platform counted 435 million users. By 2019, the number had grown to 660 million—pretty much an increase of 50 percent in a short period of time.

Diversity Is a Key Success Factor

Where do you start? Diversity seems like an ocean of opportunities for companies to improve their performance, yet 41 percent of managers in the United States feel[133] "too busy" to implement relevant initiatives.

The New York Times[134] took a deeper look into the statistics when it comes to diversity in leadership positions: "The Top Jobs—Where Women Are Outnumbered by Men Named John" was the headline of an article that looked at female representation in various organizations:

----

133 https://builtin.com/diversity-inclusion/diversity-in-the-workplace?

134 https://www.nytimes.com/interactive/2018/04/24/upshot/women-and-men-named-john.html

There are fewer women among …	…than there are men named:
CEO of Fortune 500 companies: 5%	James: 5%
Republican Senators: 12%	John: 14%
Democratic Governors: 13%	John: 19%

If all women in a certain position in total are less than a single name of all males, you know that things are not good at all.

At the same time, employees have a clear expectation: 57 percent[135] think their companies should be more diverse, most likely because they know better what works better. Josh Bersin[136] stated back in 2015 that gender-diverse companies are 15 percent more likely to outperform their peers, and ethnically diverse companies even excel at 35 percent. Bersin added, "Companies that embrace diversity and inclusion in all aspects of their business statistically outperform their peers."

> To develop soul supporters, it is critical for global companies to really understand the drivers of outperformance when building successful teams.

Adobe, the number one firm on the 2021 Soul Index, has introduced its aspirational Adobe for All program to represent an ideal version of the company. It focuses on a safe and inclusive workplace, a commitment to racial justice, progressive benefits, employee communities, and programs designed to make everyone feel appreciated.

Various studies confirm that gender diversity is critical—comparing least gender diverse companies with most gender diverse results in a significant advantage gap for diversity. Gender diversity is one element, but

----

135 https://builtin.com/diversity-inclusion/diversity-in-the-workplace?
136 https://joshbersin.com/2015/12/why-diversity-and-inclusion-will-be-a-top-priority-for-2016/

ethnic and cultural diversity play a similar role. Diversity is a key driver for business outperformance—and the members of the workforce often see it while their leaders seem to have a hard time accepting it. Again, it's the shared behaviors inside an organization that allow companies to build or rebuild corporate soul.

To develop soul supporters, it is critical for global companies to really understand the drivers of outperformance when building successful teams. The numbers indicate that more and more firms are understanding this, but the level still remains low for now.

Key thoughts to consider on rewards, including fair pay, for soul supporters

	Soul Searching in Action
✓	Do your employees personally experience that you value them as much as your customers?
✓	Do your employees think their performance is linked to the company's shared purpose?
✓	Do you review performance and compensation for the different staff levels on a regular basis?
✓	How much attention does your leadership team give to the lower ranks of staff?
✓	Do you have programs in place that address cost of living challenges of lower rank individuals?
✓	Does your back-office staff feel the value they bring to the business?
✓	Is employee engagement measured and reviewed by rank in your company?
✓	Are you aware of the diversity levels at different ranks of your company?

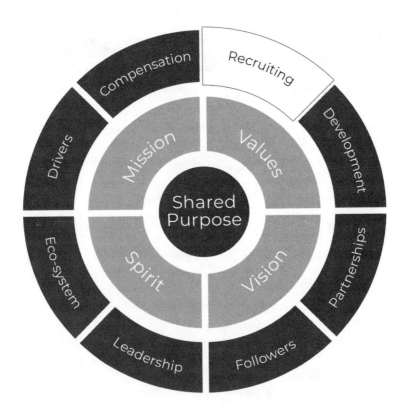

Figure 17: Recruiting as a critical component within the shared behaviors of the Soul System™.

CHAPTER 9

Hire Soul Makers

How can you hire people who fit at every level into the organization—and strengthen it for the benefit of all?

Chapter Goal:
- - - - - - - - - - - - - -

Understand the importance of diversity and inclusion to increase performance—and how to leverage behavioral interviewing to really understand who you are about to hire when it comes to finding the needle in the talent haystack.

"We are in a war for talent"—ever since the early 2000s that phrase has been used a million times. But what does it really mean? Is it *talent* in the *Merriam-Webster* sense only? It defines talent as "a special often athletic, creative, or artistic aptitude" or "general intelligence or mental power."[137] Well, all of that is correct—but is it enough to define talent in the sense of building corporate soul?

- - - - - - - - - - - -

137 https://www.merriam-webster.com/dictionary/talent

Jim Stengel's book *Grow*[138] identifies "building the business culture around the ideal" as critical for the success of outperforming companies the world over. He writes, "The heart of organizational culture is how you deal with human resources issues. If you don't hire, train, interact with, manage, promote, and reward your people based on your ideal, you will never bring the ideal to life for consumers." So, all critical human resources capabilities are not just about talent as a resource for functional capability, but also a critical lever to make the shared purpose of the company become reality. Not just by doing what is expected, but also by delivering it in a way that is in sync with the way the company or brand wants to be perceived.

It goes without saying that when you want to ensure that your company maintains the corporate soul that has made it so strong, you want your people to know how to hire soul makers—the right talent that will live up to that soul. That means finding people with good or strong emotional intelligence[139]—which is the capability of individuals to recognize their own emotions and those of others, discern between different feelings and label them appropriately, use emotional information to guide thinking and behavior, and adjust emotions to adapt to environments. This is a critical factor when it comes to hiring people—but it hasn't been a priority for many companies so far.

Annie McKee, a senior fellow at the University of Pennsylvania and an executive coach at Fortune 500 companies, researched this topic and published her findings in the *Harvard Business Review* in an article titled "How to Hire for Emotional Intelligence."[140] Her research shows that mostly people hire for intellect. "One of the reasons we see far too little emotional intelligence in the workplace is that we don't hire for it," she writes. "We hire for pedigree. We look for where someone went to school, high grades

- - - - - - - - - - -

138   Jim Stengel. *Grow: How Ideals Power Growth and Profit at the World's Greatest Companies.* New York: Crown Business, 2011.

139   Andrew M. Colman. *A Dictionary of Psychology* (3rd ed.). Oxford University Press, 2008.

140   https://hbr.org/2016/02/how-to-hire-for-emotional-intelligence

and test scores, technical skills, and certifications, not whether they build great teams or get along with others. And how smart we think someone is matters a lot, so we hire for intellect."

We have all seen this. A potential hire has an impressive resume and the right credentials, and we believe this is the right person. But how often have we failed? How often did we bring in the wrong person? They might have had all the factual ingredients, but they did not connect with colleagues and clients.

Understanding the Concept of Emotional Intelligence

At the end of the last century, a body of literature began to emerge centering on the notion of a potentially more vital competency and predictor of organizational and personal success. Rooted in emotion, empathy, and self-awareness, three scholars, Mayer, Caruso, and Salovey, introduced the concept of emotional intelligence. In doing so, they created a large movement of thinking, at times controversial, but certainly profound in its implications for how organizations are led.

Others soon contributed to their idea, notably Daniel Goleman, who popularized the approach in his New York Times best-selling book *Emotional Intelligence* (1995). The success of Goleman's book propelled both interest and opposition to the thinking, especially from those who viewed the concept as a fad and not academically grounded. Even so, Goleman added to the thinking with a five-part model for emotional intelligence springing from Mayer, Caruso, and Salovey's work. Goleman asserted that the asset of one's "intelligence quotient" (IQ) would be insufficient for future leaders. Technical skills, he offered, would give way to one's emotional quotient (EQ) in the determination of future leadership success. His five-part model included the following:[141]

----

141 Daniel Goleman. *Emotional Intelligence*. New York: Bantam, 1995.

1. Self-awareness: knowing one's emotions, strengths, weaknesses, and drives

2. Self-regulation: managing one's emotions and being equipped to adapt emotionally

3. Social skills: the middle ability to identify and manage others' emotions

4. Empathy: the ability to recognize and consider others' emotional states

5. Motivation: the ability to recognize, understand, and consider others' feelings

PSD Instead of PhD

When he joined Porsche as the global sales and marketing director back in 1994, Hans Riedel was faced with a company on its knees. Yes, there was a brand halo from the past—but a sales result of only 11,700 cars that year spoke volumes. When he left Porsche 12 years later, sales had increased by more than 700 percent. The company had undergone a complete turn-around through a swift and sustained deployment of the principles of lean production, lean management, and lean thinking across the firm. The power of the Porsche brand equity worldwide that we know today was Riedel's masterpiece. It is not only this phenomenal success that created his reputation as the icon of premium luxury car marketing. He shared with me his secrets of success when it came to hiring and building a team.

"First of all: I have always interviewed every candidate not just for the direct report level but also one level below. We had to build a team from scratch and that meant we needed individuals who were compatible with one another. Too often had I seen great minds not being able to collaborate effectively," Riedel said.[142]

- - - - - - - - - - -

142 Hans Riedel, in an interview with the author, 2020.

When your company requires an atmosphere of breaking up "traditional" approaches, ensuring your teams are able to work together toward a common goal is critical. Riedel ensured that the probability of this happening was high by one simple approach: a unique way of defining hiring criteria. "Poor, Smart & Driven = PSD" became the outline for his approach to hiring his direct reports and theirs. "Where are you coming from, what´s in your head and do you really want to accomplish big things—these were the three questions to which I required a sound response. If not, there was no way you could join the team. But if you did, then you were ready to get on board," he said.

Searching for individuals who were really hungry for success became a principle that helped Porsche build a great team in sales and marketing to drive the growth of this world-class brand. But it was not just the shared desire for success that was critical. It was also the fearlessness with which his associates were equipped: "I was searching for intrapreneurs, people who were not afraid to fight for the right thing—even if they had to put their job on the line," Riedel said. Intrapreneurs are defined as employees who are given the freedom and financial support to create new products, systems, and services while not having to follow the company's usual routines or protocols.[143]

Riedel wasn't looking for anarchists, but for the mammoth task ahead, he required great minds that were *imbued with soul* to accomplish the shared objective. Not only did he assemble a team that helped create the success Porsche subsequently enjoyed, but he also created a spirit that became infectious throughout the entire company. It comes as no surprise that not everybody in the company was convinced that it was really possible to accomplish the mission that was set out. But the management qualities of Riedel and his colleagues created an environment—a culture—that enabled the team to lead people to achieve what they did not believe possible.

- - - - - - - - - - -

143 https://en.wikipedia.org/wiki/Intrapreneurship

The characteristics of this approach still apply today: Under the heading of "Who we are," Porsche defines its critical principles on its website: "We're pleased to say that our employees are proud to work at Porsche. They are driven by passion for our extraordinary products. That motivates them to constantly seek improvements, and to regularly examine and optimize structures. Our employees sometimes think in unconventional ways, and Porsche supports this because we value independence and individuality."[144]

The company refers to its founder, Ferry Porsche, and the willingness to go the extra mile in driving a culture of tradition and innovation. At the same token it sets the bar high on financial performance: "We also expect extraordinary results when it comes to the profitability of our company." The company is proud of its performance culture but at the same time believes the fair treatment of fellow employees is the prerequisite of strong performance—it is a strong example of a company that has built and is continuing to build its corporate soul. Similar to LinkedIn (Microsoft in 2016), Porsche was acquired by Volkswagen in 2012. Both acquirers have found a way to let the corporate soul of their acquisition remain intact.

Thus, independence and individuality, two key characteristics of the Porsche brand, are mirrored in the shared behaviors of the company's employees—and in what the company looked for in new employees. This is how you build corporate soul.

Hiring on Behavioral Traits

When we hired for our start-up company Spark44, we were focusing 100 percent on behavioral traits. We had a mammoth task ahead of us with a growth plan to be operational around the world in just four months from signing the agreements. We needed real pros—but with an attitude. How did the person deal with failure? What did they need to prove to the world

144   https://www.porsche.com/international/aboutporsche/jobs/employer/values/

(whatever the world was—sometimes it was just themselves; sometimes it was previous teams and colleagues)? It did wonders—but we saw a lot of examples when we grew too fast and our first-line leadership was not capable of managing that process in the desired way that was true to our corporate soul. The lesson learned was clear: We needed to get better in how we interviewed candidates to increase the "right in soul" number.

Annie McKee suggests, "Behavioral event interviewing is not magic, and it takes practice to get enough detail in each story. Don't worry about asking the person to go back over portions of the story a time or two. Rather, try to get them to tell you the story from a couple of vantage points—what he thought, what he felt, and then what he actually did. Take your time: this is not the kind of interview you can do in half an hour. But the time is well spent. If you're able to 'see' your candidate's EI [emotional intelligence] in action, you'll make a better hire. Or you'll pass. Either way you're doing yourself and your organization a big favor."[145]

I have been involved in hiring talent for over twenty-five years and learned a great way during this time. During my early years at McCann-Erickson, there was a paradigm that was always in the room when the conversation got into any kind of business, predominantly when it came to client matters. The agency had perfected the way to handle international accounts and considered itself the undisputed leader in this space. "Refuse to lose" was the mantra that all of us got infused with. Losing business was not an option—for twenty-two years I was proud to be involved with working with companies like Coca-Cola, Nestlé, Microsoft, and many more. But even when a business got lost for whatever reason, the leadership did not give up and tried to win it back. Sometimes it took years to do it—but the option to not try the very best was just not in people's minds. And when you got into the hiring mode, you always remembered to hire for both the functional capabilities required and for the esprit de corps that was galvanized into that "refuse to lose" attitude.

----

145 https://hbr.org/2016/02/how-to-hire-for-emotional-intelligence

Finding the Cultural Fit

During the start-up phase of Spark44, the founding team studied the human resources practices at Zappos, a billion-dollar online shoe and clothing shop based in Las Vegas. It's also one of Fortune's Top 100 Best Companies to Work For. When we set up the firm, we needed people who embraced change, understood and motivated colleagues and clients alike, and were able to deal with all the emotions that came with the turbulent times when you start a new enterprise. We hired people who wanted to make history—the desired turnaround of the Jaguar brand was what got us there. But the intellectual capability was not enough— managing a start-up advertising consultancy that was geared to support the transformation of a multibillion-dollar automotive business required talent with a unique mix of passion, resilience, and everlasting energy to strive for the best possible solution and take their clients and teams with them—no matter what obstacle was put in the way. Why did we look at Zappos then?

Learning from Zappos meant understanding the importance of the "cultural fit." If candidates have the right skills but are not a good fit with your company's core values, they should not get the job. Period.

At the 2013 START conference, Zappos CEO Tony Hsieh made this point crystal clear in his speech: "We've actually passed on a lot of really smart, talented people that we know can make an immediate impact on our top or bottom line, but if they're not good for the company culture, we won't hire them for that reason alone." Zappos's philosophy is simple: *Deliver happiness to customers, employees, and vendors, and profits would be taken care of.* Hsieh and his team designed ten (the initial list included thirty-seven!) core values that make Zappos "Zappos":[146]

- Deliver WOW through Service

- Embrace and Drive Change

----

146 https://www.zappos.com/about/what-we-live-by

- Create Fun and a Little Weirdness

- Be Adventurous, Creative, and Open-Minded

- Pursue Growth and Learning

- Build Open and Honest Relationships with Communication

- Build a Positive Team and Family Spirit

- Do More with Less

- Be Passionate and Determined

- Be Humble

When Amazon.com acquired Zappos in 2009, no change was applied. Its independent management structure ensured that the culture would not be touched. With the majority of its staff being call center agents, the company can control the voice of the brand. Zappos is exceptional at this. A special team trains the entire staff on those core values. So every employee hears the same message, learns the values, and practices the behavior that is expected to live the values every day at work.

It is not unusual for a recruitment process at Zappos to take months between the initial cultural fit interview via an HR recruiter and the actual job offer. While it is standard practice that a number of employees meet potential candidates, Zappos ensures that the candidate interacts with Zappos's employees in social settings, too. That could be a department or company event. So even those who are not involved in the formal process will have a chance to meet the candidate. But any candidate only gets there when they have passed the cultural fit interview successfully. It counts for 50 percent of the decision; the other 50 percent is obviously about the capability fit. But candidates can only get to the second 50 percent—meaning they do get to meet the hiring manager and other employees—once their fit to the culture is confirmed.

How do the interviewers get the right sense of whether the candidate does fit the culture? There are a few behaviorally based questions that shine a light on the candidate's fit to the company's core values. But it goes beyond the interview conversations. As we all know, a lot of people "act" in a job interview. Figuring out if it is their real self is a difficult task. At Zappos they use a simple but powerful way to understand whether the personality they met was the real personality—or if there was another side to them. "A lot of our candidates are from out of town, and we'll pick them up from the airport in a Zappos shuttle, give them a tour, and then they'll spend the rest of the day interviewing," Hsieh said. "At the end of the day of interviews, the recruiter will circle back to the shuttle driver and ask how he or she was treated. It doesn't matter how well the day of interviews went, if our shuttle driver wasn't treated well, then we won't hire that person."[147] Getting real feedback from real people is a great way to get a real picture of a person. Whether it is the shuttle driver, the receptionist, the assistant—if people's values matter, these people can give you a real sense of how they felt interacting with that candidate.

The core values indicate that the "Customer Wow" is critical to Zappos. To ensure that every new hire gets it, they have to spend the first month in the call center. This is where they learn how to respond to customer needs. Organizational culture expert Billy Selekane believes this is heavily connected to the soul of the company: "While this is an introduction to the soul of the business, it is also a practical approach to serving customers all year long."[148]

But then comes the piece that got Zappos the most public interest when people learned about it in the first place. Once new hires complete their call center phase, they are offered $2,000 to leave the company.[149] Why? Zappos believes that the first month is enough time for any new

----

147 https://www.businessinsider.com/tony-hsieh-zappos-hiring-strategy-2013-11

148 https://www.linkedin.com/pulse/20-ways-zappos-reinforces-its-company-culture-billy-selekane-csp-hof/

149 https://medium.com/@dperciv1/why-zappos-pays-people-to-quit-7912260b1fe5

hire to become a fully committed member of the Zappos community. If the new hire feels that the job isn't really for them, then Zappos offers them this amount to leave. Once they take it, they can never come back, though.

Zappos perfected their approach and found a way that fits their purpose and most likely builds corporate soul through it. But the Zappos way is the Zappos way. Every company has to find their own way—if they are serious about their shared purpose, their shared understanding, and their shared behaviors.

This is the real deal—and as a leader you have to lead in an uncompromising way to make this real. It takes effort to get there. Ensuring there are important milestones that manifest the culture is critical. For us at Spark44 there were a few:

- "Sparkapalooza," our festival of innovation once a year in every office

- "The Larry's," naming our employee evaluation system in the name of Larry Uniac (he was the greatest vocal believer in the strength of these evaluations, and we named the evaluation after him when he passed away far too early)

- "Be Bold, Be Brave, Be Honest," our mantra that reinforced the permission to think and act with passion, conviction, and humility in everything we were doing

- "Finca," which were our executive off-site meetings named by the type of location (anything but a normal hotel) to ensure the location would inspire the creative spark that galvanized the entire organization

- "SparkBnB," the two-month exchange program for employees into another office

Culture Fit or Culture Add?

While hiring for cultural fit is one of those approaches that is hard to say no to, it is really tough to get done in real life. Patty McCord, a human resources consultant and former chief talent officer at Netflix, told *The Wall Street Journal*,[150] "What most people mean by culture fit is hiring people they'd like to have a beer with. You end up with this big, homogenous culture where everybody looks alike, everybody thinks alike, and everybody likes drinking beer at 3 o'clock in the afternoon with the bros." But that is not what it is all about. It is about creating a values-based performance culture—one that is driving real value. So what does it take to get it right?

Amelia Sordell,[151] founder of the personal branding agency KLOWT, has a thought-provoking view on this subject: Stop hiring for culture fit and start hiring for culture add. "By searching for and filtering in people with exactly the same values and ideas as your existing team, you can not only stunt your company's growth, but you can actually create an environment where outside ideas are stamped out and innovation dies," she said, echoing McCord's opinion.

Sordell introduces a thought that is critical: "You need to start matching candidates to your aspirational culture, not your current one." Unless the current culture matches the aspirational one, which only very rarely is the case, every hire provides an opportunity to close the gap to the aspirational culture. Plus—obviously—it offers an opportunity to create better and stronger products or services through accelerated innovation cycles.

If the values are understood and lived, the culture will emerge on its own. Lars Schmidt, founder of Amplify, a human resources agency that helps companies navigate the new world of work, discussed the leading team collaboration and productivity provider Atlassian, which was at the time

- - - - - - - - - - -

150   https://www.wsj.com/articles/the-dangers-of-hiring-for-cultural-fit-11569231000

151   https://www.linkedin.com/pulse/stop-hiring-culture-fit-start-add-what-how-utilise-amelia-sordell/

reframing its approach to reducing unconscious bias: "Their values fit inter-viewers are carefully selected and given training on topics like structured interviewing and unconscious bias. They're also given a set of behavioral questions to assess whether a candidate would thrive in an environment with their company values: a dedication to transparency, empathy towards cus-tomers and colleagues, and initiative to drive positive change."[152] As a result, Atlassian has been able to increase the share of female members of their workforce, as well as attracting more people of color.

Aubrey Blanche, global head of Diversity & Inclusion at Atlassian, is very clear on what it is all about: "Focusing on 'values fit' ensures we hire people who share our sense of purpose and guiding principles, while actively looking for those with diverse viewpoints, backgrounds, and skill sets. We're trying to build a healthy and balanced culture, not a cult."[153] Again, fully understanding and living the values allows the culture to thrive.

> **To create a values-based performance culture, hiring soul makers is paramount.**

To create a values-based performance cul-ture, hiring soul makers is paramount. It is critical that—as in the Zappos example—everybody on the team understands the company's purpose and buys wholeheartedly into it. That includes the work ethics that are at play and the way decisions are being made by leadership *and* are being received by staff.

Take the Time for a Real Reference Check

It is a reality in the hiring process that managers often spend little time with the candidate. But even if you take your time and have multiple sessions with the candidate during the recruitment process, it will always only be a snapshot in a somewhat artificial environment of interviews.

152, 153 https://www.linkedin.com/pulse/end-culture-fit-lars-schmidt/

That is where references come in. I am not talking about those written one-pagers full of praise—I am talking about a real conversation (i.e., talk with them) with a previous manager of the person you are aiming to hire. They have spent months or years with the candidate and can offer many more facets to understand whether your final candidate is the right one: How did the candidate behave in real life? How did they treat colleagues at the same level or at higher or lower levels? How did they operate with customers?

But reference checks can work both ways. The anticipation of a candidate who names a reference is usually "that person knows me well and regarded me highly so they will recommend me for the job I want." But because the previous manager does know the individual so well, they can also provide valuable insight to the candidate on whether the potential next employer really would be a good fit.

I remember when one of my leadership team members decided to leave—in a very amicable way. She had contributed a lot, and a few months later, she called me up and asked whether I would be a reference for her. Of course, I said. A week later a call was scheduled with her potential new boss, the CEO of a fintech start-up. During that call, I was able to provide him with all relevant information—much to his delight. But when we hung up, I felt I needed to call her. Everything that CEO told me between the lines had directly made me think, "Is this the right environment for her?" So, I called her the next day and shared my thoughts—as I knew that she was successful at our company because the values and the mission and the purpose were so close to her heart, and it seemed that there wouldn't be that fit with that potential new employer. I told her, "This might be quite a stretch for you!" She was quiet for a moment and then said, "I am so happy that you are that open with me—it's been bothering me for quite a while, but I was not sure whether this would be a fit. Hearing from you the same concerns that were going through my mind helps me in making my decision: I won't go there!" This was probably not the outcome that any of the three of us had expected, but it shows how important reference checks are in finding the right fit.

Hire to Retire

One can argue forever and ever whether it is a good thing or not if an employee spends their entire career within one company. That is not the point of this provocative heading—rather look at it from the perspective of career growth within a company based on a strong purpose with aligned shared understanding and shared behaviors.

Let's take a look at Hilton. In a People Matters interview,[154] Lara Hernandez, Hilton's senior vice president of Human Resources in the Asia Pacific, shared interesting insights on the company's talent management strategies. "At Hilton, we believe in creating what we call the 'hire-to-retire' experience for our Team Members—a seamless experience from the beginning, which enables access to a multitude of opportunities and skill sets within the organization," she said. "This means being present at every step of the journey, from ensuring that they have a great experience through the recruiting process and all the way through the onboarding period and beyond. It is also about making sure that our Team Member benefits are regionally and culturally relevant."

Since Hernandez has been around the hospitality industry for more than two decades across all continents, she is aware of the differences in local cultures that need to be synchronized with the corporate culture. Her responsibility across the Asia Pacific region includes talent development for over 50,000 team members. She sees her role as a business partner to the organization "enabling the building of a strong culture focused on robust purpose-led talent strategy."

The Hilton definition of a "business of people serving people" is also the North Star when it comes to managing benefits that make a difference in a specific culture. "In China, our female general managers who move away from their families for work are given relocation support and monetary aid to assist in covering their children's school fees, so

----

154 https://www.peoplemattersglobal.com/article/employee-relations/we-believe-in-creating-
hire-to-retire-experience-for-our-employees-hiltons-sr-vp-hr-22673

Soul makers can come from anywhere—not just in terms of their previous position or employer.

that they are able to remain together as a family," Hernandez said. "As we grow exponentially across the region, these aspects in turn become increasingly important as our workforce expands to include a multitude of Team Members from diverse backgrounds and cultures."

Diversity and Performance

Soul makers can come from anywhere—not just in terms of their previous position or employer. They can literally come from anywhere in terms of ethnicity, geography, or gender. As we saw in chapter 8 in developing soul supporters, diversity is a key driver of performance.

Soul Index 2021 winner Adobe has very systematically approached that topic through their Adobe for All program. They have identified four key areas[155] to drive greater diversity and inclusion:

- Building the talent pipeline. The tech industry faces a dilemma in many countries globally: Not enough women and members of underrepresented groups are pursuing tech careers. It's an industry-wide challenge. Hence, Adobe cooperates with Braven, a non-profit organization that backs college students from underrepresented backgrounds on their path to strong first jobs and economic freedom. Adobe is also a founding member of the Reboot Representation Tech Coalition whose aim is to double the number of Black, Latina, and Native American women graduating with computing degrees by 2025.

- Attracting diverse candidates. Adobe works to ensure inclusivity and fairness in their sourcing, interview and hiring processes,

---

155 https://www.adobe.com/diversity/strategy/industry.html

and they have activated their Adobe Digital Academy to help non-traditional candidates transition to careers in tech.

- Enhancing the employee experience. All the previously mentioned efforts don't help if employees leave the company after a short time. Community-building, training and internal awareness-building, family-friendly policies, and parity commitment are the key pillars to an extraordinary experience, as the strong results in key rankings confirm.

- Driving diversity across our industry. Adobe is committed to drive a diversity and inclusion agenda with their customers, partners, vendors, and peers through a number of initiatives. They do support the Sundance Ignite program to enable the next generation of filmmakers with a year of mentorship. In 2020, the Women at Sundance–Adobe Fellowship was launched to help female filmmakers launch successful and sustainable careers.

These efforts are guided by aspirational goals[156] for overall representation and representation at leadership levels for employees. Adobe wants to increase representation of women in leadership positions to 30% globally by 2025: their 2020 diversity report says that in 2020, the number was 26.1%. Given the fast-growing history of the company, this already is quite a task. The following table shows that the company is well underway in the Americas, Europe, and the Middle East, as well as the Asia-Pacific region and Japan, since the promotion rates for women in 2020 were already higher than for their male colleagues across these regions.

In 2018, Adobe achieved something that many companies have either just defined as a goal or are not considering important enough to take action: equal pay. After a two-year effort, the company achieved

----

156 https://blog.adobe.com/en/publish/2021/04/20/diversity-inclusion-year-in-review.html

pay parity between male and female employees. By September 2020, the firm announced pay-parity among US-URM (Under Represented Minorities) and non-URM employees. This is a great result that makes Adobe a real role model for 21st century companies. They define pay parity[157] "as ensuring that employees in the same job and location are paid fairly relative to one another, regardless of their gender or ethnicity." This is something the leadership team around CEO Shantanu Narayen can really be proud of.

	Americas	India	EMEA	APAC + Japan
Overall	16.2%	24.6%	13.9%	13.4%
Women	17.8%	23.9%	16.0%	14.2%
Men	15.4%	24.8%	13.0%	13.0%

Table 5: Adobe 2020: employees with internal promotions overall and per gender

The Workforce Demands It

These diversity efforts by Adobe are truly important, not just to increase the performance of the company, but also to increase its attractiveness as an employer. Remember, this chapter started with a reference to the war for talent. With aging societies in the West, that war is real. Companies need to look at their employer brand when they make decisions about their future approach. The employer brand is synonymous with the reputation of the employing company as a place to work. Employees increasingly have a choice to make up their mind about what is their next preferred employer. The younger they get, the more demanding their

- - - - - - - - - - -

157 https://www.adobe.com/diversity/parity/overview

criteria. The Deloitte Millennial Survey[158] was published in 2020 when the COVID-19 pandemic had already spread across the world. The study states, "Millennials who feel their employers are creating diverse and inclusive work environments inched up three percentage points from last year, to 71%. 'Having a positive impact on communities' improved (65% to 69%)." These numbers look promising—even with the caveat that millennials chose their employers with the idea of diversity and inclusion in mind. The Deloitte survey suggests a number of initiatives that can further improve the employer brand:

- Showing a commitment to making the world a better place for everyone and demonstrating a purpose beyond profit

- Addressing climate change and implementing environmental sustainability programs

- Providing community engagement opportunities for employees

- Ensuring diversity and inclusion across the organization, and promoting compensation structures that reduce income inequality

- Making employee mental health a priority

To do justice to these findings, it is essential for companies to review their hiring process. When it comes to ensuring that the hiring process does not leave talented individuals out because of their gender or their ethnic origin, having hiring decisions rooted in emotional intelligence is key to avoiding those unconscious biases.

The Interview Process

Every company needs to define its killer interview question to figure out whether the candidate is a potential soul maker. For Netflix,

----

158 https://www2.deloitte.com/cy/en/pages/about-deloitte/articles/millennialsurvey

the question was simple: Were they interested in the company's goal of making the customer happy? Netflix's Patty McCord offered this straightforward perspective: "The best hires find the company's business goals motivational."[159]

Whichever way you look at it, the process of hiring needs attention and structure—too many managers are not trained well enough to manage this correctly. The list of criteria for structuring an interview provided by Amelia Sordell is very comprehensive:[160]

- How do we conduct interviews? If it's a panel, what are the roles and backgrounds of the panel members?

- What questions do we ask at the interview? How do we score candidates' answers?

- What supplementary questions do/could we ask?

- What is the potential impact a hiring manager's unconscious bias could have? What are we doing to mitigate it?

- What environment do we interview in? What is the room layout? Do we provide refreshments and a warm welcome to all?

- Are we rejecting overqualified candidates? Why?

- As a company, where do we want to be? Can this candidate help us get there?

- What are our blind spots?

- Is our company structure the right environment for this candidate?

- What work environments do they know to allow them to reach their maximum potential? Can we facilitate this?

- - - - - - - - - - -

159   https://www.wsj.com/articles/the-dangers-of-hiring-for-cultural-fit-11569231000

160   https://www.linkedin.com/pulse/stop-hiring-culture-fit-start-add-what-how-utilise-amelia-sordell/

- Does this person have transferable skills that could supercharge our mission?

- What inspires candidates? What energizes them?

- What are this person's interests? Communication style and ideas? Do they differ from our own? Will their approach challenge our current working culture?

With a solid structure in place, that brings us back to emotional intelligence and how to apply it to the interview process. In her *Harvard Business Review* article on emotional intelligence,[161] Annie McKee concludes that basic self-awareness and social skills often are rare in the leadership area: "They don't recognize the impact of their own feelings and moods. They are less adaptable than they need to be in today's fast-paced world. And they don't demonstrate basic empathy for others: they don't understand people's needs, which means they are unable to meet those needs or inspire people to act."

She refers to both research and the commonsense notion that "people who understand and manage their own and others' emotions make better leaders"—and presumably better interviewers.

From my own experience, I have several recommendations that can help to get the most out of every interview:

- Banal, but true: Be on time; don't let the candidate wait.

- Have a room that allows for no disturbance during the interview.

- Start with questions to understand the background of the person's resume or CV.

- Get into the behaviors outside the interview space (i.e., let the person share a challenging situation in their current job and

---

161 https://hbr.org/2016/02/how-to-hire-for-emotional-intelligence

how they fixed it—ideally find out about the dynamics that were at play to understand the context of the work situation).

- Ask about what the person learned from this experience.

- Find out what the person would have done differently, either in solving the challenge more quickly or easily, or even avoiding the challenge in the first place.

- Don't stop asking until you are satisfied with the answer. Often candidates don't go deep enough in their responses.

- Change the context from challenges to successes. Let the person share their biggest success and explain the dynamics that allowed it to happen.

- Give the candidate a sense of importance by sharing a related story from your company and watch the reactions carefully.

- Final question: Move back to an unsuccessful situation and let the candidate explain to you how they dealt with it.

- My recommendation is to also bring a second observer into the conversation, especially if you are not a very experienced interviewer. It always helps to have an observer who is able to listen and observe at the same time. It can be difficult to do both when you are the one conducting the interview.

In McKee's view it is critical to learn about how the candidate "thinks in situations that involve stress, challenges, and other people." This allows you to really get a sense if the environment you are offering is the right place for that person. Take your time. It is worth it, and an extra hour invested here can save you a lot of time and money, as well as mental energy later, if you were to find out you made the wrong decision.

McKee offers her set of dos and don'ts around emotional intelligence (EI) to apply during the hiring process:[162]

- - - - - - - - - - -

162 https://hbr.org/2016/02/how-to-hire-for-emotional-intelligence

Do:	Don't:
Get references and talk to them	**Use a self-report test**
Letters of reference simply aren't good enough when it comes to understanding your candidate's EI. When you actually talk with a reference, you can ask specific and pointed questions about how the candidate demonstrated various EI competencies. Get lots of examples, with lots of detail. Specifically, ask for examples of how your candidate treats other people.	There are two reasons these don't work. First, if a person is not self-aware, how can he possibly assess his own emotional intelligence? And if he is self-aware, and knows what he's missing, is he really going to tell the truth when trying to get a job?
Interview for emotional intelligence	**Use a 360-degree feedback instrument**
This sounds easy and many people think they are already interviewing for EI. But we aren't, much of the time. That's because we allow people to be vague in their responses and fail to ask good follow-up questions. Even when we ask candidates directly about EI or EI-related competencies, they talk about an idealized notion of themselves and what they'd like to be, rather than how they really behave. To overcome this obstacle, you can use behavioral event interviewing.	Even if it is valid and even if it measures EI competencies, like the Emotional and Social Competency Inventory does. A tool like 360-degree feedback ought to be used for development, not evaluation. When these instruments are used to evaluate, people game them by carefully selecting the respondents, and even prepping them on how to score.

Table 6: Annie McKee's dos and don'ts in hiring for emotional intelligence.

Hiring soul makers is a real craft and like any craft needs training and experience. It really pays off in the long-term. Imagine you are able to identify the right candidate who buys into the soul of your business and helps you to build it forward. Hallelujah!

Key thoughts to consider on hiring soul makers

	Soul Searching in Action
✓	Have you defined the personality criteria or soft skills for any new hire?
✓	How often do you personally make a reference check when it comes to key hires?
✓	Do you really understand what drives a person who wants to work for you?
✓	Have you considered giving new hires extra pay if they come to the conclusion that they don't really fit the culture?
✓	Are you clear about what the new hire adds to your culture?
✓	Whose input do you consider when setting up interviews outside the hiring manager and the HR colleague?
✓	What role does diversity play when you are hiring?
✓	Is your company ready for the future workforce?

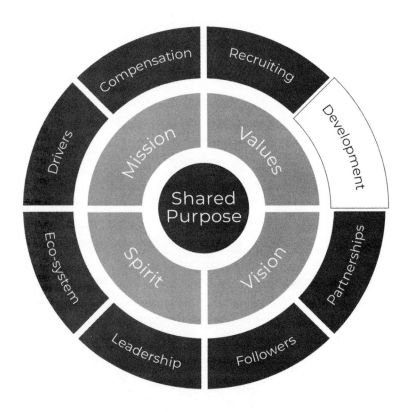

Figure 18: Leadership development as a critical component within shared behaviors of the Soul System™.

CHAPTER 10

Grow Soul Leaders

How can you ensure that your lower-level soul supporters
and drivers can build their careers in your organization?

Chapter Goal:
- - - - - - - - - - - - - -

Understand the importance of what it is that creates
personal fulfillment for your future leaders, as well as who
is considered a leadership role model in your company.

Upon my departure as CEO of Spark44, one of my associates,
Ronja Schütt, had this to say: "Thank you for your continued belief in me. Thank you. I have accomplished things that
I never even thought I was capable of. Thanks to Spark44 . . . I have
become a leader. You have given me the trust and the dance floor. You and
your partners have achieved something incredible." These words touched
me deeply—and they confirmed that we had created a very unique culture of performance, shared trust, and belief, coupled with the hunger
for doing the unprecedented. Our mantra was "We empower people to
challenge conventions so that amazing things happen." That element of

empowering people allowed us to create a culture of fearlessness—combined with a belief that it was the ultimate responsibility of management to allow people to grow inside the organization.

By building a foundation upon which soul supporters can develop their careers in your organization—as Spark44 did for Ronja—you are creating an atmosphere where they can become not only ambassadors for your shared purpose but also leaders for your company.

In studying the success of Hilton, I came across a great example of a leader who gets it: Iriana Formato, director of catering and events at the Hilton Chicago O'Hare and Rosemont hotels. Featured in a Hilton case study by Great Place to Work˚, Formato had been at different Hilton hotels for over fourteen years before she came to lead a team of about twenty members. She started her leadership role in the usual way—by getting to know her people. But she did not stop at the surface. She learned about each person at a deeper level so she could understand "what their goals are, what makes them tick, what makes them happy, and what helps them thrive."[163] While that would still be something you would expect of a passionate leader, she has taken this to a different level: "I constantly have 1-on-1s," Formato says. "Everybody's motivation is different. You need to get to know them on a personal basis."

This building of trust with her team is commonplace among Hilton's leaders. According to Great Place to Work˚, "some 84% of individual contributors at Hilton say their leadership shows 'a sincere interest in me as a person.'" This is exactly the response that an organization that has built corporate soul recognizes as a "we are on the right track" statement.

Again, it is all about empowering people in the workplace; I felt the same when I received an email from a former Spark44 employee, Thibault Plantet. His email to me when the news broke about my stepping down was heartwarming and reflected on the time that this young advertising expert and I worked together. I had been able to convince him to leave his great job in Paris and move to Frankfurt—and then again only three

- - - - - - - - - - -

163 https://www.greatplacetowork.com/images/reports/2018-GPTW-Profile-Series-_Hilton_ Hospitality_For_All.pdf

years later I offered him an opportunity to move to São Paulo. Thibault wrote, "I grew, as a professional and as a person. I remember you came back from a business trip to Brazil, and I exchanged with you a few words in Portuguese. I saw the light of opportunity in your eyes. Because that's what you do. You understand people, and you develop them. You trusted me. You sent me as the Spark44 representative to Brazil. I was stressed by the responsibilities and honored and did my best because you put your trust in me. . . . The way you trust your team, is something I'll keep in my heart as an inspiration for my entire life."

According to Great Place to Work*,[164] Hilton is creating this kind of leadership culture at scale: "When such a behavior across the entire organization is happening, the whole organization benefits. . . . For All Leaders builds strong bonds of trust with their direct reports, fosters strong ties within their team and across the wider organization, and regularly reinforces the company's mission for team members. . . . And they are devoted to the development of their people."

The Interdependence between Fair Promotions and Continuous Feedback

Promoting from within, as discussed in chapter 7, and using good hiring practices (chapter 9) are both ways to get and retain good employees, but beyond those processes, how companies can nurture and empower their employees to grow in their roles and realize their potential as soul leaders is a key question. Soul leaders are critically important. But let's make no mistake here: Every employee—every soul driver and soul supporter (chapters 7 and 8)—is equally paramount. This is an essential insight since not every employee wants to become a leader, but that doesn't mean they don't want to grow in their jobs either.

How can you ensure that your non-executive-level soul supporters and drivers can build their careers in your organization—as future leaders or

- - - - - - - - - - - -

164 https://www.greatplacetowork.com/images/reports/2018-GPTW-Profile-Series-_Hilton_
     Hospitality_For_All.pdf

not, as the case may be? Like in many other areas of life, communication is the answer. How can you learn what moves, bothers, worries, or excites your team members if you do not talk *with* them? Not just talking *to* them, talking *with* them.

This sounds very simple and, in a way, straightforward, but in reality, it is not. The significance of feedback in career development is an essential responsibility of every line manager. The corporation needs to ensure that this is managed well by providing both the tools and understanding for how to do it. Culturally, the familiar phrase "I've got something more important to do" needs to become an unacceptable sentence. Examples like Thibault speak volumes to the power of this approach.

The Great Place to Work˙ documentation shares another example of how this approach to talent coaching is happening in real life. The case study highlights Hilton employee Andrew Dixon, the executive chef at the Doubletree Crystal City in the Washington, DC, area. Dixon has thirty-five direct reports and enjoys seeing his staff progress in their careers even if it means they leave Hilton, like a former sous chef at the Doubletree who went on to become an executive chef at a local restaurant. "That's how I judge my success as a leader, and that is what drives me," Dixon said. In his previous workplaces, he experienced little to no staff development, but that has been vastly different at Hilton. "They want to know what my goals are," he said. "That's one of the things that keeps me at Hilton."[165] By taking the time to seriously listen to its staff, Hilton has helped develop leaders within the organization like Dixon, who in turn are doing the same for their staffs.

The Andrew Dixon example represents a company-wide approach that has taken the sense of belonging into new spheres. According to Great Place to Work˙, nearly 90 percent of all individual contributors "report they are treated as a full member of the Hilton community, regardless of their position."

- - - - - - - - - - - -

165   https://www.greatplacetowork.com/images/reports/2018-GPTW-Profile-Series-_Hilton_Hospitality_For_All.pdf

Grow Equals Thrive

Hilton's talent management strategy is driven by its value proposition, Thrive@Hilton. This umbrella theme includes a variety of initiatives that allow employees to grow in body, mind, and spirit. In its *Team Member Guide*,[166] Hilton CEO Chris Nassetta provides a simple logic as the bottom line for the program: "We're excited to invite you on this journey, because when you thrive, Hilton thrives."

One module focuses on mindful leadership, which is directly linked to leadership, one of the Hilton values: "Our organization defines leadership as the ability to inspire and motivate people so that they achieve the impossible. At Hilton, everyone is a leader." The module connects practical tips with

> "Our organization defines leadership as the ability to inspire and motivate people so that they achieve the impossible. At Hilton, everyone is a leader."

the company's leadership development framework, which provides all owned and managed hotel and corporate team members with opportunities for leadership development within three distinct tracks based on the employee's level.

Program	Target Group	Job Titles
Elevate	Emerging Leaders	Individual Contributors / Entry-Level Managers
Engage	Established Leaders	Managers through Senior Directors
Excel	Enterprise Leaders	GMs, VPs, SVPs, EC

Table 7: Hilton's mindful leadership structure.

----

166 Thrive@Hilton, *Team Member Guide.*

This creates a transparent approach for everyone in the company. Being selected as a leader is obviously one thing, but the Thrive@Hilton program is geared toward everyone inside the company, providing growth opportunities for all.

Great Bosses Recognize Great Talent

During my career, it has always been the greatest joy when a member of my team made it to the next level. I have always taken a lot of pride in the career progress of my colleagues as it showed that they were ready for the next level. Leticia Thenard is a great example to illustrate that point. I hired her in 2014 to be the single point of contact for Brazil and Latin America at Spark44. She gave up her job at a renowned agency because she was convinced by the vision that I shared with her at the time. Our business grew and grew—to a point where we had to manage a team of twenty individuals. Leticia had displayed her entrepreneurial and leadership skills during all aspects of that growth period. I did not have the slightest sense of doubt that she would be able to become the managing director of that operation. Her farewell message to me condenses this point in a nutshell: "I will never forget what you have done for me, and all the trust you had in me and in my work. If you had asked me in my first interview if I felt prepared to all the challenges we had, I think I would have said that I was not the right person and that I couldn't make it. But because of you and all the trust you had in me, we made it . . . so you are the kind of leader that makes us accomplish things that we don't even know we are capable of."

Sydney Finkelstein, who is the Steven Roth Professor of Management at the Tuck School of Business at Dartmouth College, published a great article a few years back in the *Harvard Business Review* titled "What

> "You are the kind of leader that makes us accomplish things that we don't even know we are capable of."

Amazing Bosses Do Differently."[167] His research provides five different behaviors that are key to managing teams effectively and hence creating a platform for associates to grow:

- Manage individuals, not teams.

- Go big on meaning.

- Focus on feedback.

- Don't just talk . . . listen.

- Be consistent.

These five points may feel obvious. But they are not what is happening out there. A 2013 Society for Human Resource Management survey of managers in the United States found that "only 2% provide ongoing feedback to their employees." Just 2 percent! When we introduced quarterly evaluations plus mandatory team lead and employee conversations, this was something new to many of our staff, and most of our people had to learn how to give feedback in a proper fashion. At our company it was not 2 percent but 100 percent of our managers around the globe.

As I mentioned earlier, talking *with* and not talking *to* is the critical aspect. When our company grew exponentially and it was no longer possible to talk with everyone regularly, the conversations with individuals that were highlighted as great contributors in the evaluation discussions with my direct report provided so much insight into what was happening at the ground level. That allowed me to take key actions

> Talking *with* and not talking *to* is the critical aspect.

that the staff would not only accept but also endorse as they were seeing that their thoughts and suggestions were actually taken seriously. And there were moments when this was the most critical thing. When we went through a significant restructuring, Neil Cassie—who wrote the

---

167 https://hbr.org/2015/11/what-amazing-bosses-do-differently

foreword to this book—coached our leadership team to ensure we would get through this in the best possible way. I still remember his words after interviewing with the leadership team and key contributors: "Stay who you are in this phase. You have so much credibility for your integrity with everybody inside the company, and you'll get through it. They know it will be tough, but they also know you will handle it in the fairest way possible."

Culture Matters—Being Aware of Differences Among Countries

Understanding the cultural nuances in talking with employees or expressing criticism within your feedback is a key skill as well. Different cultures may have different approaches to expressing their views and opinions. Latin cultures are more enthusiastic; in the United Kingdom there are more polite ways to say "it does not work" than in probably any other country; and in the Asia Pacific, hierarchical status is so important that it creates challenges in conducting open and honest conversations. But regardless, that is no excuse to not do it.

When it comes to the international workplace, research findings by the O.C. Tanner Group[168] are very helpful for these organizations, as it allows them to compare the market sentiment against a number of relevant criteria for key markets around the world. The methodology for this study is quite sophisticated (multi-method research design combining employee interviews, focus groups, cross-sectional surveys, and a longitudinal survey). Qualitative finds were derived from 16 focus groups (Denver, Toronto, London, Sydney) and 108 interviews, as well as 20,888 online survey interviews with workers at companies with 500-plus employees across the world.

- - - - - - - - - - -

168 https://www.octanner.com/global-culture-report.html

O.C. Tanner Organizational Culture Research 2020

	USA	CDN	MEX	BRA	ARG	UK	GER	RUS	SAA	IND	UAE	CHI	JPN	SIN	AUS
Employee Sense of Purpose	73%	70%	72%	75%	68%	68%	68%	63%	70%	82%	70%	70%	56%	70%	74%
Employee Sense of Opportunity	65%	60%	71%	74%	63%	57%	59%	55%	60%	83%	67%	70%	47%	68%	66%
Employee Sense of Success	68%	65%	72%	75%	64%	60%	62%	61%	65%	83%	51%	68%	47%	68%	70%
Employee Sense of Appreciation	62%	58%	65%	68%	59%	55%	57%	62%	60%	70%	64%	67%	51%	64%	62%
Employee Sense of Well-Being	57%	55%	60%	60%	56%	51%	50%	54%	53%	46%	51%	55%	51%	50%	52%
Employee Sense of Leadership	62%	57%	64%	68%	57%	55%	57%	54%	56%	74%	63%	65%	44%	63%	62%
Employees are engaged	74%	68%	76%	78%	73%	67%	68%	62%	74%	84%	74%	69%	51%	68%	75%
Employees would leave for another job with similar role, pay and benefits	57%	46%	66%	60%	42%	54%	55%	47%	53%	75%	63%	66%	49%	60%	64%
Employees are satisfied with their current workplace culture	71%	69%	78%	77%	72%	64%	64%	65%	64%	84%	64%	74%	49%	68%	71%
Employees feel a sense of burn-out	43%	54%	31%	35%	60%	48%	44%	40%	46%	45%	42%	35%	50%	44%	45%

Table 8: O.C. Tanner organizational culture comparison across selected countries provides nuance of the priorities that employees are considering when evaluating their workplace culture.

The good news: There are more similarities than there are differences. Table 8 shows the six senses of an employee—a compelling approach as it provides interesting clusters of countries with similar patterns. Take the Employee Sense of Appreciation, for instance. If a manager did continuous feedback rounds, I am sure that the percentages would most likely be higher than the midfifties to midsixties.

Employee Sense of Purpose: When employees agree to that statement, their work takes on meaning. Most countries fall between 68 percent and 75 percent of employees feeling a strong sense of purpose. That is surprisingly high—but India tops it with 82 percent. Anyone who has ever worked in India knows why—a relatively young workforce that is eager to perform. Japan having the lowest percentage (56 percent) is no surprise either; the strong sense of belonging—in many cases lifelong—to the same employer is heavily anchored in the workforce.

Employee Sense of Opportunity: This aspect states how employees view the chance to develop new skills, contribute to meaningful work, feel challenged, have a voice, and grow. India rocks again. The closest countries percentage-wise are Brazil, Mexico, and China. Every other country ranks below 70 percent, with Japan being at the end of the league table with only 47 percent.

Employee Sense of Success: This is a very critical component as employees must find success at the individual, team, and organizational levels. Again, India and Japan are the two ends of the spectrum. In between the two, it is very homogeneous between 51 percent and 70 percent.

Employee Sense of Appreciation: This aspect describes the feeling of being valued for one's contributions and being recognized for one's worth. Not surprisingly, India is at number one and Japan has the lowest percentage—but lower scores also appear for the United Kingdom, Canada, and Germany, with everybody else being in the midsixties.

Employee Sense of Well-Being: This looks at how employees think about the level of caring the company provides to employees as a whole—their physical, emotional, social, and financial health. That is the one criterion where India moves to the lower end of the league table. Only 46 percent of employees have that sense of well-being. It is no surprise to me given the salary levels and social systems in this giant country. I have seen many people working so hard for very low wages and salaries, and the stress that these individuals have in taking care of their families must be immense. The highest scores are to be found in Mexico and Brazil. But make no mistake: 60 percent is enough to top the table, as everywhere else the numbers are in the midfifties. Basically, everywhere in the world, only half the employed population feels a sense of well-being. When you look at the numbers on "Employees feel a sense of burn-out," it is worrying to see that Argentina (60 percent), Canada (54 percent), and Japan (50 percent) claim the stress is taking its toll. But make no mistake, the numbers are disturbing everywhere else too: always in the midforties except for the "best"—Mexico (31 percent) and Brazil and China (both 35 percent).

Employee Sense of Leadership: This looks at the leaders who provide the mentoring, coaching, inspiring, and facilitating that creates environments of collaboration and support. India is back on top, and Japan is back at the end of the league table. Six countries don't even make the 60 percent barrier: Canada, Argentina, the United Kingdom, Germany, Russia, and South Africa!

These results indicate a significant impact on employee loyalty. The killer question from the survey is, "Employees would leave for another job with similar role, pay and benefits." The most loyal employees can be found in Argentina (42 percent) and the least in India (75 percent), where employees would turn to the next opportunity right away. Beyond Argentina, the only other countries where loyalty is above 50 percent are Canada, Japan, and Russia. Everywhere else it is less.

The *2020 Global Culture Report* is just the second one that O.C. Tanner has released. Their conclusion is sound: "To create a better overall employee experience, organizations need to evolve beyond the limitations of the life-cycle view, and focus on high-impact, daily micro-experiences instead. These experiences connect employees to the cultural norms, values, and behaviors that add up to a thriving workplace culture. That culture, in turn, creates a strong, sustained influence on engagement levels, productivity, innovation, and many other core metrics of success." Across the board, the numbers got better in 2020 compared to 2019 (see figure 19).

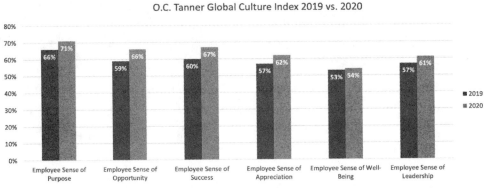

All scores have increased between 4 and 7 percentage points except "well-being" (only 1%).

Figure 19: O.C. Tanner Global Culture Report YoY comparison.

It will be interesting to compare the 2021 numbers and beyond when the impact on workplace culture will be noticeable with long-term home office arrangements plus significant unemployment or furlough measures that have been applied across the world during 2020.

> There is nothing wrong with *building team soul,* but it won't add up to *building corporate soul* when it is not designed against a common corporate approach.

O.C. Tanner concludes the findings from its report by saying, "To continue substantial culture gains, organizations need to pursue a cohesive strategy that deliberately connects culture efforts with employee experience initiatives."

They see organizations becoming more intentional about improving workplace culture, identifying their target states, and beginning to address deficiencies and problems. Often, though, culture initiatives are siloed, and strategies are fragmented, leading to wide disparities in the employee experience. There is nothing wrong with *building team soul*, but it won't add up to building *corporate soul* when it is not designed against a common corporate approach. Only a shared purpose, supported by a shared understanding and shared behaviors across an entire organization, can accomplish this.

Employee Experience vs. Employee Life Cycle

The work from O.C. Tanner is really groundbreaking as it offers a methodology to focus on the employee. Traditionally, HR departments have been focusing on the employee life cycle—which is definitely not the way employees look at what is happening. According to O.C. Tanner's research, 92 percent of employees describe their employee experience as their *everyday experience*. It is not the shiny perk, the great off-site meeting once a year—it is what it is: their day in the office, in the warehouse, in the delivery van, behind the counter, or whatever their profession might be.

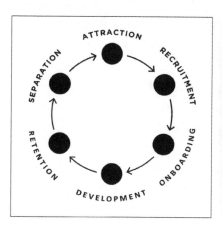 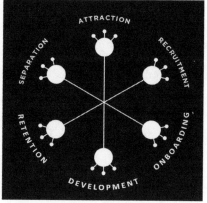

EMPLOYEE LIFE CYCLE

The traditional corporate view of the employee experience involves six distinct career stages known as the employee life cycle.

EMPLOYEE EXPERIENCES

To foster a positive work environment, HR leaders design programs to deliver employee experiences around each life cycle stage.

Figure 20: O.C. Tanner employee life cycle vs. experience graphic.

The *2020 Global Culture Report* states,[169] "Employees are thinking of their personal experiences—a collection of thousands of interactions they have in an organization, both positive and negative. Every conversation they've had, email read, poster seen, appreciation received (or not received); how they are treated by leaders; how easy or difficult it is to get resources, answers, and information. What employees experience is not the once-or-twice-a-year HR initiative, but all the micro-experiences they encounter each and every working day. Only 42% of employees would rate their employee experience as positive or extremely positive."

In the context of the Soul System™, the employee experience is critical. Behaviors of colleagues and managers drive that experience big-time. If these behaviors are somewhat erratic, it is very difficult for an employee to consider themselves as part of a tribe of that corporation. But if companies apply the logic of shared understanding and shared behaviors, they will start looking at their employees as ambassadors of the soul of their company and not just as "a means of production and profit, as evidenced by the term 'human resources.'" Again, when you look at the O.C. Tanner research, the business impact of getting it right is more than obvious since they have been able to differentiate between thriving and non-thriving corporate cultures.

The Soul Index has already proven that companies with corporate soul perform significantly better than their peers. Figure 21 shows the impact thriving cultures (synonymous with companies with soul) have on key drivers of success: Employee engagement has a factor of 13— what a result! Or a factor of 7 on innovating. Last but not least, a factor of 2 (which means *doubling*) is for those cultures to have likely grown their revenue.

----

169   https://www.octanner.com/global-culture-report.html

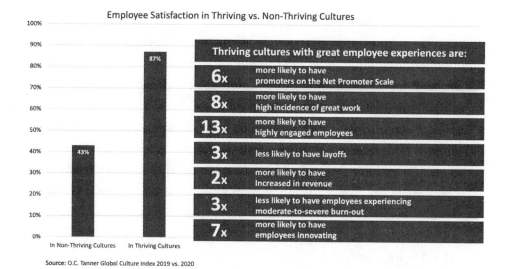

Source: O.C. Tanner Global Culture Index 2019 vs. 2020

Figure 21: O.C. Tanner impact of thriving cultures.

Personal Fulfillment—A Soft Factor with Hard Impact

Chapter 7 looked at the importance of a great manager and their impact—positive or negative. That in and of itself can make or break a business. As mentioned in the section "Great Bosses Recognize Great Talent," the impact managers have on employees is significant. But let's be clear: While this impact is significant, it should not be taken as a carte blanche excuse for nonexistent job fulfillment. Sometimes one has to realize that their chosen firm is just not the one. And act.

ReWork cofounder Nathaniel Koloc said,[170] "Let go of the idea that careers are linear. These days, they are much more like a field of stepping-stones that extends in all directions. Each stone is a job or project that is available to you, and you can move in any direction that you like. The trick is simply to move to stones that take you closer and closer to

---

170   https://hbr.org/2013/08/build-a-career-worth-having

what is meaningful to you. There is no single path—but rather, an infi-
nite number of options that will lead to the sweet spot of fulfillment."
Koloc describes himself as "an entrepreneur and strategist committed to
supporting ventures, projects, and people who are working to ensure that
the future arrives safely for our society and our planet."

A mission-driven search firm, ReWork stewards a national network of
exceptional professionals who are building meaningful careers by working for companies that are making social, environmental, and cultural
progress. In 2019 ReWork became part of Koya Leadership Partners,
providing a comprehensive resource for mission-focused executive search
and talent needs.

What Koloc calls fulfillment, O.C. Tanner calls employee experience,
but while O.C. Tanner's aim is to help employers change their perspective,
Koloc wants employees to approach their career by seeking "legacy, mastery, and freedom—in that order."

The order is important. Legacy stands for the higher purpose, mastery
indicates the art of getting better and better, and freedom equals the ability
to choose what you want to do with whom you want to do it.

In Koloc's experience, there's a reason why some people are successful in finding—and maintaining—a fulfilling work approach: "They treat
their careers like a *grand experiment*." He explains why he uses the word
grand, which you rarely find in publications around career management: "I
use the word 'grand' to describe this experiment because the reality is that
your career is not just a way to earn a living. It's your chance to discover
what you're here for and what you love. It's your best shot at improving the
world in a way that is important to you. It's a sizeable component of your
human experience, in a very real way. As such, it should be an adventure,
with a healthy bit of magic and mystery along the way. So, if you're one of
the many who find themselves on the path to meaningful work—remember to enjoy the journey, don't give up, and don't settle."

For a leader, supporting their associates on their career path is also
grand—it is one of the most fulfilling experiences. After a few decades

in leadership positions, I am still overwhelmed when I meet former colleagues who remember our conversations even today. For them, I was *the* leader, *the* manager, *the* boss who helped shape their career. For them, it was one of *these* moments that gave them the next idea or a context that they had not thought of themselves. It is the most satisfying leadership moment. More than that, it is the fuel that helps leaders to identify and grow soul leaders. When I saw the following poster on a LinkedIn post,[171] I thought, "It says it all."

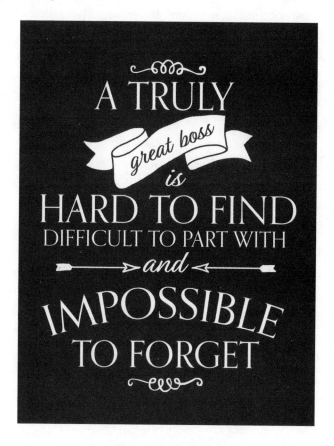

Figure 22: A great boss.

----

171   https://www.linkedin.com/pulse/choose-boss-job-supports-you-trusts-believes-make-oleg-vishnepolsky/

Successful Companies Grow Leaders

"Only 13% of companies say they do an excellent job developing leaders at all levels"—this is the opening statement of LinkedIn's guide "Developing Employees Into Leaders."[172] It is a worrying statistical figure as it means that nearly nine out of ten companies have issues developing their key people. That is what makes a perfect business case for head hunters the world over. But looking at the logic of shared purpose, shared understanding, and shared behaviors, companies should be able to do better. Unless they do a very poor job in recruiting in the first place, there should be a better ratio of developing leaders than 1:9.

But we have all seen it. It is a mindset issue. Very often, companies do not incentivize internal career management as well as they could to really develop employees into leaders. Managers find "good reasons" why they cannot support an employee moving to another level, department, country, or what have you. The result is that employees have to walk away and find another company—and often you hear these anecdotal stories of "I would have really liked to stay, but they did not offer me that next step. I could have created that much value."

The 13 percent figure that LinkedIn has identified is a huge concern when you consider the generational changes in workforce structures that are ahead of us. According to the LinkedIn guide, "These challenges are particularly important as older leaders retire at accelerating rates and millennials assume leadership roles. According to *Forbes*, millennials will comprise 75 percent of the workforce by 2025. Millennials are no longer the leaders of tomorrow—they are rapidly becoming the leaders of today."

LinkedIn has identified three dynamics that drive successful leadership development:

1. A healthy talent pool of engaged employees

----

172 https://learning.linkedin.com/content/dam/me/learning/EMW/lil-guide-developing-employees-into-leaders.pdf

2. Robust training that actively develops that talent

3. A culture that identifies and promotes employees from within

The most critical one is the third. Many companies have that healthy pool and robust training in place. But if the culture that identifies and promotes from within is nonexistent, the investment in the pool and the training do not yield the return that was desired. Incentivizing leaders to support the growth of their potential successors is key.

When we started Spark44, we founders sat in a room writing on a flip chart all the behaviors that we did not want to experience in our new company. As we evolved, stories like the one of Thibault or Ronja became the norm—be it intercultural moves or fast-track growth inside the company. But it started with a flip chart—where we put up the leadership deficiencies we had seen in our careers before. As we grew, it became obvious that we needed to strengthen our leadership base.

To assist our people to have the confidence and the skills needed for this quest, I turned to an expert in the field of leadership and emotional intelligence: Kevin Allen. His work provided a great base for what we had to do—hiring soul makers as mentioned in chapter 9. He wrote a bestseller on emotional motivation and launched an exciting company, E.I. Games, delivering emotionally intelligent leadership training in a highly engaging online game-based format that checked the box on all three levels—being globally scalable, highly creative, and engaging. We launched this wonderful simulation all across our network where participants role-played the CEO of a troubled company called Planet Jockey where they were challenged to make emotionally intelligent leadership choices for thirty-five management dilemmas, all while being harassed by an evil company called Wolf Industries. It was great to see how our people got into it and drew parallels from certain situations in the game to their everyday reality. They loved it, and the language of emotional intelligence began to circulate all around the company as participants in various meetings began to notice. I suppose one of our employees in Shanghai put it best: "It was love at first click."

Kevin Allen is still at it with a multitude of business games now all around the globe at companies like Google and Oracle and universities like Arizona State and the Harvard School of Design.

Role Models Wanted

Every one of us has met individuals during our career that are "hard to forget" as they inspired us in what we were doing and where we were heading. Sometimes, people find their role models inside their existing company, but sometimes they meet them in other surroundings. Indeed, a leading worldwide employment-related search engine, lists these traits of effective role models in the workplace:[173]

- Accountability
- Hard work
- Positivity
- Persistence
- Integrity
- Respect

All of these characteristics sound very noble—and there might be many other attributes that individuals consider relevant for their role model. But no matter which attributes are relevant, role models are critical for the growth of employees in the workplace. Indeed shared five key functions and benefits for why these traits are important:[174]

1. **They increase employee morale.**
   They simply help to make the nine-to-five life more enjoyable. Morale is on the rise when role models are around. Role models are an inspiration to their coworkers.

173, 174 https://www.indeed.com/career-advice/career-development/role-model

2. **They inspire healthy competition.**

   They really lift the bar. I have often seen a role model in a group significantly improve the quality of work shared at the next level.

3. **They create a positive atmosphere.**

   When morale is on the rise, atmosphere wins. There are more smiles and high fives around. But not as a replacement for great work—as a result of great work.

4. **They motivate others.**

   Make no mistake: Role models appreciate an easy life. But they know the way to get there is to coach and mentor their colleagues to enable them to get to better results faster. A classic win-win situation.

5. **They communicate openly.**

   By definition, inspiration comes from sources outside yourself. Role models are happy to share their ideas. As Indeed reveals, "They are willing to communicate with their employees and coworkers about how they became skilled and successful in their job roles. For instance, the supervisor of a role model may ask about specific feedback on a new process their company has implemented, and a role model would give honest and positive feedbacks and offer perceived alternatives to fix any potential issues with the new process—always in a respectful and helpful way."

Growing soul leaders is really one of the greatest gifts to a leader—if they are prepared to accept it. Finding the right way in a corporate environment and in a cultural sphere is something that I have always enjoyed the most. Both personally but also from the viewpoint of the success of the company.

> Growing soul leaders is really one of the greatest gifts to a leader—if they are prepared to accept it.

Key thoughts to consider on growing soul leaders

	Soul Searching in Action
✓	Do you know the ratio of leaders who have grown from within or from the outside of your company?
✓	Are you able to contextualize local cultural nuance when growing future leaders?
✓	Can you express what it is that creates personal fulfilment with your future leaders?
✓	Have you discussed the issues you have in identifying future leaders with your management teams and taken actions?
✓	Who are the role models for future leaders inside your company?
✓	Is your executive team aware of the impact opportunity when growing future leaders?
✓	How good is your team with pumping up potential future leaders with confidence?
✓	Have you put a future leaders roundtable in place?

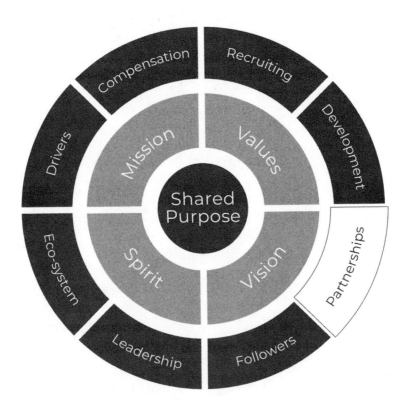

Figure 23: Defining appropriate partnerships as a critical
component within shared behaviors of the Soul System™.

CHAPTER 11

Identify Soul Allies

How can you enter into partnerships with corporations and communities that think and act alike?

Chapter Goal:
- - - - - - - - - - - - -
Understand the role of corporate social responsibility in the context of building corporate soul and aligning it fully with your company's environmental, social, and governance approach.

As a matter of course, corporations are maintaining partnerships with other organizations—whether these are mere sponsorship arrangements or commercial activities such as creating joint venture entities or other forms of collaboration. A multitude of criteria is usually applied when it comes to forming these partnerships: Do we have successful shared experiences with one another? Do we share the same passions? Is this an opportunity to expand our business network? Can I trust the other partner? Do they apply a great level of creativity in their dealings? Do we share the same vision?

The last question is extremely important when you have your company's Soul System™ in mind. Like-mindedness of vision and values is the make-or-break criteria for selecting partnerships—*soul allies*—when your company is working on building its corporate soul. It might be the top athlete and the performance brand, the great artist and the luxury brand—you name it. But that is a mere marketing exercise—often with a short- or medium-term perspective. There is a reason for those, but that is not the subject of this chapter. This is about the long-term perspective. This is about the behavioral side of purpose, the activities that allow soul to turn into a halo, one that is a long-term reflection of the purpose of the company.

> A partnership should underline the reason why your company matters: to all stakeholders and society as a whole.

A partnership should underline the reason why your company matters: to all stakeholders and society as a whole. Over the past years, more and more corporations have started relationships with civil society organizations (CSOs) such as environmental initiatives, local clubs or think tanks, or nongovernmental or governmental organizations like UNICEF or WHO. Multi-stakeholder organizations or federations of all kinds are being considered as well.

As we discussed in chapter 6, Patagonia is known for getting its purpose "right" as shown in its dedication to environmental causes. Founder Yvon Chouinard recognized early on that his company could have an impact in protecting wild places and established a 1 percent giving program in 1985 that donates 1 percent of sales to the preservation and restoration of the natural environment. Since then, the company has awarded more than $89 million to domestic and international grassroots environmental groups making a difference in their local communities. Patagonia has also found those key value partnerships to help widen its 1 percent program's impact. In 2002 Chouinard partnered with Craig Mathews, owner of Blue Ribbon Flies, to create the nonprofit organization 1% for the Planet, which encourages other businesses to also give 1 percent of their sales to environmental causes. Since then, more than 3,000 enterprises have joined. Patagonia's partnership with Blue Ribbon Flies thus has been a perfect fit and to the benefit of the global environment. Mathews and his wife, Jacquelyn, founded Blue Ribbon Flies, a fly shop based out of West Yellowstone, Montana, in 1980. The Mathewses have dedicated their lives to conservation efforts and fly-fishing, as well as supporting many other conservation organizations.

Although he retired from operational roles in Patagonia by 2020, Chouinard felt the COVID-19 pandemic required him to make a very clear statement to the 1% for the Planet community:[175]

> I've never celebrated Earth Day. I've always felt that all of that attention on just one day distracts us from the need to be taking action for the planet every day.
>
> But these are extraordinary times. This pandemic is showing us clearly that if we put off what needs to be done, it ends up coming back to bite us. We've known for a long time that there would be a global pandemic, and we've done nothing. We've known for decades about global warming, and we've done nothing. We've got to choose to act.
>
> As members and nonprofit partners of 1% for the Planet, you have made that choice. And during this challenging time, it's not an easy one. But it's the right one. When Patagonia has faced hard times before, as we are now, the absolute last thing that we would give up is our 1%. It's a cost of doing business on this planet. It's not philanthropy—it's an absolute necessity for us living on this planet. It's the opposite of doing nothing.
>
> It's also so important that we stay in this together. One lesson that I've learned, and that this pandemic is certainly

----

175 https://www.onepercentfortheplanet.org/stories/a-letter-from-yvon-chouinard

teaching us, is that we're not in isolation. The problems we're facing now have to be solved on a global basis, and can only be solved by people working together and staying tough together—like all of you in the 1% for the Planet community.

So, hang in there, stay the course, and remember that this community matters during these extraordinary times and at all times.

My thanks to all of you for your commitment. It means a lot.

—Yvon

Founder of Patagonia & 1% for the Planet

P.S. Remember, vote the assholes out—all of those politicians who don't believe we should do anything about climate change. Vote for the planet and against those who would do nothing. We have the power and now is the time to use it.

Patagonia's environmental efforts are not an "add-on" corporate social responsibility activity but an organic extension of the firm's purpose. In fact, its partnerships with nongovernmental organizations and like-minded companies that share its perspective on protecting the environment are a strong example of the power of corporate social responsibility in today's world—when done for the right reasons.

Corporate Social Responsibility

Wikipedia defines corporate social responsibility[176] (CSR) as a type of international private business self-regulation[177] that aims to contribute to societal goals of a philanthropic, activist, or charitable nature by engaging

---

176 https://en.wikipedia.org/wiki/Corporate_social_responsibility

177 Benedict Sheehy. "Defining CSR: Problems and Solutions." *Journal of Business Ethics.* 131, no. 3 (Oct. 2015): 625–648. doi:10.1007/s10551-014-2281-x. ISSN 0167-4544.

in or supporting volunteering or ethically oriented practices.[178] While it was once possible to describe CSR as an internal organizational policy or a corporate ethics strategy,[179] that time has passed as various international laws around CSR have been developed and various organizations have used their authority to push CSR beyond individual or even industry-wide initiatives. While CSR has been considered a form of corporate self-regulation for some time,[180] over the last decade or so it has moved considerably from voluntary decisions at the level of individual organizations to mandatory schemes at regional, national, and international levels.

In summary, CSR has been there forever—but it has changed its face over the years. The Social Purpose Institute calls these CSR 1.0, 2.0, and 3.0:[181]

- **CSR 1.0**: This first iteration centered on the idea that because companies don't exist in isolation from the world, they should do good things to contribute to it.

- **CSR 2.0**: This version introduced the concept of creating shared value—that doing good could align with a company's overall business strategy—and potentially add revenue.

- **CSR 3.0**: The latest evolution involves a more integrated approach that aligns a company's business strategy with the power of its social network.

It is fair to say that for both CSR 2.0 and 3.0, the sustainability reports that are now required by law are as relevant as the United Nations Global Compact and the United Nations's seventeen Sustainable Development

----

178   Nancy Lee; Philip Kotler. *Corporate Social Responsibility Doing the Most Good for Your Company and Your Cause.* Hoboken, NJ: Wiley, 2013.

179   https://www.cbsnews.com/news/business-ethics-integral-to-corporate-strategy-says-stanfords-malhotra/

180   Benedict Sheehy. "Understanding CSR: An Empirical Study of Private Regulation" (PDF). Monash University Law Review (2012).

181   https://socialpurpose.ca/social-purpose

Goals (SDGs), which were adopted by all UN Member States through the 2030 Agenda for Sustainable Development[182] in 2015. These public reports have created significant visibility for CSR activities. This has led more companies to ensure that their CSR activities are really thoughtful and a key component of their business strategy.

Purpose-Led Sponsorship— A New Trend or Just a Fig Leaf?

Sponsorships come with many risks, which becomes blatantly obvious when reading sponsorship contracts. The obvious risks are well known. For example, in the world of sports, doping is a key issue. One of the most prominent examples has been Nike's endorsement of Lance Armstrong. Nike's mission is "what drives us to do everything possible to expand human potential,"[183] which is the opposite of using performance-enhancing drugs.

One of the biggest endorsement fails in recent history is the 2017 Pepsi activation, which depicted model and TV star Kendall Jenner. The commercial became news across the world and is a prime example of how the attempt to leverage a social and political cause can go fundamentally wrong. Jenner's role in the commercial was to reduce tensions between protesters and police by handing a Pepsi to a police officer. Social media— and "real" media—reactions were very similar: The commercial essentially trivialized sensitive topics like Black Lives Matter, racism, and police violence. Pepsi's vision to be "Winning with Purpose"[184] sounds great, but this way of bringing it to life failed miserably. The ad was pulled immediately.

Thus, you must be sure you're forming a partnership for the right reasons. Since purpose has become a hot topic, the event and sponsorship

---

182 https://sdgs.un.org/goals

183 https://about.nike.com/#:~:text=Are%20An%20Athlete.-,About%20Nike,where%20 we%20live%20and%20work.

184 https://www.pepsico.com/about/about-the-company

industry has started to identify campaigns linked to their clients' corporate purposes. The European Sponsorship Association has added a "Purpose-led Sponsorship" category to its annual awards structure. Two categories are up for grabs: "Cause" and "Sport." *PRWeek* magazine started its Purpose Awards in 2019.[185] The 2020 shortlist shows the general importance corporations are giving to this topic: "As studies consistently show that consumers want brands and companies to take a stand on certain issues, purpose has never been more important. PRWeek's second annual Purpose Awards highlights the brands, companies, agencies and individuals doing the best job at putting purpose at the forefront of everything they do." There's a myriad of categories *PRWeek* offers:

- Best Advocacy
- Best B2B
- Best Collaboration
- Best Environmental
- Best Equity & Inclusion
- Best Fundraising
- Best Health
- Best Integration into Culture
- Best Proof of Authenticity
- Best Public Awareness
- Best Use of Celebrity and/or Influencers

- Best Use of Creativity
- Best Use of Digital/Social Media
- Best Use of Technology
- Best Student Campaign
- Most Purposeful Person Under the Age of 30
- Most Purposeful Agency Pro
- Most Purposeful In-House Communicator
- Most Purposeful CEO
- Brand of the Year
- Agency of the Year

Table 9: *PRWeek*'s categories of Purpose Awards 2019.

If you look through the list of selected winners, it feels as if the magazine has identified a new label that is worth promoting. Many of the cases that are shown seem to only touch purpose as a marketing tactic and not as a strategic corporate activity. It mirrors the critique that advertising strategist Tom Roach shared about pseudo-purposeful brands (see chapter 3)

----

185   https://www.prweek.com/article/1691636/2020-purpose-awards-shortlist-revealed

that just see purpose as a new feel-good ad campaign about whatever social justice topic is currently trending.

NGOs Are Becoming a New Player in the Sponsoring Market

For decades, sponsoring partnerships happened mainly between large bodies in the world of sports and entertainment and their industry partners. Over the past twenty years, an increasing number of partnerships between companies and nongovernmental organizations (NGOs) have emerged. The majority are focused on a key element of the purpose of the company. By this, it becomes much more than a philanthropic approach; it becomes a key element of the business strategy that company deploys. "Traditional" sponsoring is pretty straightforward. Marketeers have perfected the criteria for how to measure the impact and define appropriate cost structures, and a whole industry of agencies and brokers has been built upon that logic. When it comes to NGO partnerships, many companies find it hard to set the appropriate goals as they are getting closer to the space that was previously looked at as philanthropy but is now becoming an element to implement the company's business strategy as part of CSR. Caroline Dale Ditlev-Simonsen,[186] a professor at BI Norwegian Business School, took a deeper look into the challenges of the industry model that prevailed for a long time, as set out in 2003 by the Boston-based consulting team of Carol L. Cone, Mark A. Feldman, and Alison T. DaSilva.[187]

---

186 C.D. Ditlev-Simonsen. "Beyond Sponsorship—Exploring the Impact of Cooperation between Corporations and NGOs." *International Journal of Corporate Social Responsibility* 2, no. 6 (2017). https://doi.org/10.1186/s40991-017-0017-9.

187 https://www.ssc.wisc.edu/~jpiliavi/965/Cone%202003.pdf

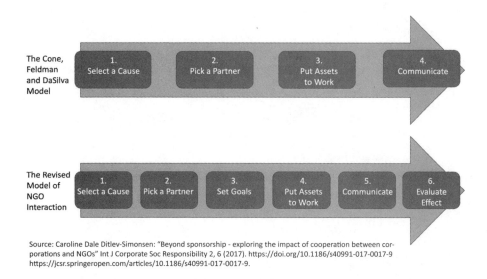

Source: Caroline Dale Ditlev-Simonsen: "Beyond sponsorship - exploring the impact of cooperation between corporations and NGOs" Int J Corporate Soc Responsibility 2, 6 (2017). https://doi.org/10.1186/s40991-017-0017-9
https://jcsr.springeropen.com/articles/10.1186/s40991-017-0017-9.

Figure 24: Comparison of models of CSR programs. Source: Caroline Dale Ditlev-Simonsen

Ditlev-Simonsen's revised model included two new elements: number 3's "Set Goals" and number 6's "Evaluate Effect." When CSR programs were basically a "do good things" activity, setting goals was usually a very lofty thing. As part of a business strategy, that changes dramatically. Why are we doing this? What is the value of every dollar we spend? These are key questions that need an answer beyond the feel-good approach of "doing good things."

Swedish furniture retail giant IKEA is a good example of a company that implements partnerships based on shared vision and values. The company's vision statement is "to create a better everyday life for the many people"[188]—everybody will agree that their "business idea supports this vision by offering a wide range of well-designed, functional home furnishing products at prices so low that as many people as possible will be able to afford them." The origins of the company can be felt in the values (full explanation of IKEA's values can be found in the appendix) they have given themselves:[189]

- - - - - - - - - - -

188 https://www.ikea.cn/ms/en_CN/about_ikea/our_business_idea/index.html

189 https://ikeafoundation.org/about/values/

- Togetherness

- Caring for people and planet

- Cost-consciousness

- Simplicity

- Renew and improve

- Different with a meaning

- Give and take responsibility

- Lead by example

IKEA has been putting its values to work through its partnerships with NGOs for decades. Let's look at its partnership with the World Wildlife Fund (WWF), for example. IKEA and the WWF formed a conservation partnership[190] in 2002 that perfectly aligned IKEA's forest action plan and the WWF's conservation targets. With the objective to "jointly promote responsible forestry in priority regions around the world," they implemented a series of projects in China, Russia, Bulgaria, Romania, Estonia, Latvia, and Lithuania. One impressive example of the impact of the partnership is the increased Forest Stewardship Council certification in Russia, which has reached 30 million certified hectares or about 25 percent of Russia's leased forests.

The WWF and IKEA cooperation[191] is based on shared values. Both organizations are committed to promoting responsible and sustainable use of natural resources for present and future needs. These projects are also an important step in IKEA becoming a more sustainable company as it implements its social and environmental strategy.

IKEA's partnerships are closely linked to what the company sells, given that its younger shoppers obviously hit the sweet spot of its target

- - - - - - - - - - - -

190   https://www.globalhand.org/en/search/success+story/document/20792

191   Ikea.com/ms/ar_JO/about_Ikea/pdf/forest_fact_sheet.pdf

consumers' environmental concerns in a very compelling way. Besides wood, one of the key materials that IKEA needs for its products is cotton. That led IKEA to again work with the WWF, as well as local organizations in India and Pakistan, on the Better Cotton Initiative to create lasting change in cotton production. Through this program, IKEA and other partnering companies have helped raise awareness of the environmental impact of growing cotton, such as the amount of water needed, and assisted local farmers in implementing more responsible growing methods. It has become the largest cotton sustainability program in the world. Since 2015, all of the cotton IKEA uses has been responsibly sourced, according to Rahul Ganju, sustainability manager for textiles for IKEA of Sweden AB. "We are committed to creating a positive change throughout the entire cotton industry," he said. "More sustainable cotton needs to become mainstream material beyond our business and we continue to collaborate and work with our partners to create an even bigger positive impact on the industry, people, and our planet."[192]

Cynics may look at IKEA's approach and argue that its furniture is not a very sustainable proposition in the first place and actually has made home interiors a seasonal item—by increasing the number of cupboards, tables, chairs, and so on that are simply thrown away after use. While IKEA's partnerships focus on the sustainability impact of the production side, the company has also launched a program to focus on the sustainability impact of the consumption side. In October 2020, *The New York Times* published an article titled "Ikea Will Buy Back Some Used Furniture" that outlined the retailer's buyback program, part of its larger efforts to combat climate change.[193] Available in twenty-seven countries, the program, which will accept back unwanted IKEA furniture, is meant to encourage customers to take a stand against excessive consumption.

- - - - - - - - - - -

192   https://about.ikea.com/en/sustainability/responsible-sourcing/committed-to-sustainable-cotton

193   https://www.nytimes.com/2020/10/14/business/ikea-buy-back-furniture.html

IKEA's buyback program is a great example of how to spread the idea of sustainability across a wide range of stakeholders. It is very sound—as both the company's partnerships and this program align perfectly with its vision and values.

Pick the Cause That Is Right for the Company in the Long Run

In the IKEA example, the causes are so well connected to the business the world's largest furniture retailer is in that there is no doubt about the fit. But often, the connection is not as clear. The Social Purpose Institute[194] provides a very comprehensive overview on what a social purpose should be—and what it is not. As the table on the next page suggests, identifying soul allies requires companies to take a long-term view and to consider their entire business model, not just a project for the next quarter. IKEA's nearly twenty years of partnering with the WWF is proof that these kinds of connections can work and support the business.

> Identifying soul allies requires companies to take a long-term view and to consider their entire business model, not just a project for the next quarter.

Brad Offman, CEO at Spire Philanthropy in Canada, is a founding member of The Corporate Partnership Conference,[195] which was first held in 2019. From his experience, being open and authentic are critical prerequisites for any successful corporate-charity partnership:

> The nature of partnerships between charities and corporations has changed dramatically over the past decade. Gone are the distinct lines between community investment, sponsorship, cause marketing and employee engagements. In order to build

194 https://socialpurpose.ca/social-purpose

195 https://thepartnershipconference.com/11-corporate-partnership-experts-on-the-most-important-trends-in-2019/

sustainable and meaningful partnerships, both sides must truly understand the objectives of the other. They must understand that successful relationships involve shared language and a candid exchange of ideas and objectives. Those engaged in partnership dialogue should not be afraid to ask probing questions and provide honest answers. Open and authentic conversations are the foundation of great corporate-charitable partnerships.

What a social purpose is not	What a social purpose should be
• A vision, mission statement, a company's values, specific business strategy or a big goal	• Core to the business model; how the company grows; driving force of the business model
• Representative of what is possible today	• Aspirational and belief-driven
• A wraparound for the company's current efforts	• Energizing and inspirational, builds momentum
• An initiative or a set of initiatives	• A way of business
• Branding, marketing, tagline, strapline, campaign or slogan, a communications device	• Constant; its story and growth strategy are one and the same
• A tactical decision	• Long-term
• An employee engagement tool	• An organizing center for the company's vision, strategy, and culture
• Supporting a social issue or the objective of the company's community investment of the corporate responsibility strategy	• Broader than the company's activities, products, or services; incorporated in the company's marketing or products
• Morality, altruism, giving back, philanthropy	• Company's commercial model
• Focused on the internal organization	• External facing, outwardly focused
• A goal or a strategy that can be achieved	• A North Star, an ongoing quest, forever pursued but never reached; it cannot be fulfilled

Table 10: The Social Purpose Institute definition of social purpose.

Partnerships in the Age of ESG

The importance of environmental, social, and governance (ESG) themes has been growing ever since the term was created in 2005. A year before, UN secretary-general Kofi Annan invited fifty CEOs of major financial institutions to participate in a joint initiative. Twenty-three institutions (representing $6 trillion USD assets under management) endorsed the initiative that was supposed to find ways to integrate ESG factors into capital markets. The 2005 report "Who Cares Wins" proved that embedding ESG factors in capital markets makes good business sense and leads to more sustainable markets and a better outcome for societies.

While environment and governance topics dominated the agenda in the early years, social topics took the spotlight during the COVID-19 pandemic. The impact of this virus amplified existing social issues in many countries around the world. According to a study by KMPG,[196] "CEOs are still very much engaged with this issue, and in particular the 'S' of ESG. Close to two-thirds (63%) said that their response to the pandemic has caused their focus to shift to the social component of their ESG program." This shift has not done any damage to their existing commitment to the "E" and "G" components of ESG: "To move forward, CEOs are looking to double-down on the structural shifts that have emerged during the crisis—71 percent say they want to lock-in climate change gains that have been realized during the pandemic. Measuring and communicating the impact of environmental improvements, as well as social and governance performance, will be critical."

To see how ESG partnerships are being implemented, let's look at LEGO. Remember that LEGO's purpose is "to inspire and develop children to think creatively, reason systematically, and release their potential to shape their own future—experiencing the endless human possibility."[197]

- - - - - - - - - - -

196 https://home.kpmg/xx/en/home/insights/2020/09/prioritizing-strategic-priorities

197 https://www.advisorpedia.com/advisor-tools/how-legos-purpose-made-it-the-most-powerful-brand-in-the-world/

When we put this into the ESG context and focus on "their own future," it becomes obvious that LEGO had to pay attention to the environmental aspects of ESG considerably—as we all know, the bricks are pure plastic. The Danish company understood that it had to take a close look at this to ensure it would maintain its relevance for current and future generations of players and shoppers, and LEGO's compliance with the United Nations Global Compact Sustainability Development Goals is well underway.[198]

LEGO's ambition is to make its bricks from sustainable sources by 2030 without compromising quality or safety. This is quite bold since it requires creating entirely new materials. LEGO entered into a collaboration with the WWF in the spring of 2015 to assess the overall sustainability and environmental impact of new bio-based materials for LEGO elements and packaging. In 2018, LEGO—using guidance from the WWF—started making a range of sustainable LEGO elements from sugarcane to create polyethylene, a soft, durable, and flexible plastic. Sugarcane grows at the same rate as it is being used and is sourced sustainably. This new material is not biodegradable as it needs to be durable and safe for generations of children, so LEGO is working with its sugarcane suppliers to meet the Responsible Ethanol Sourcing Framework, which is based on best practices. The sugarcane itself is certified by third-party standards and is third-party audited. As LEGO's website states, "It seemed only natural to make 'botanical' elements first, so we made leaves, bushes and trees—plants from plants! More than 80 LEGO elements are made from sustainably sourced polyethylene. Although these represent just 2% of the 3,600 elements available for designers, it is the first important step out of many on the journey towards using sustainable materials by 2030."[199]

LEGO executive chairman Jørgen Vig Knudstorp told *Plastics Today* that the effort was "a long-term investment and a dedication to ensuring

----

198 https://www.unglobalcompact.org/participation/report/cop/create-and-submit/
     active/437906

199 https://www.lego.com/en-us/aboutus/sustainable-materials/#:~:text=More%20than%20
     80%20LEGO%20elements,experiment%20with%20many%20different%20materials

the continued research and development of new materials that will enable us to continue to deliver great, high quality creative play experiences in the future, while caring for the environment and future generations. It is a daunting and exciting challenge."[200]

What is really impressive about LEGO is that the company has made sustainability an integral part of the corporate strategy beyond the areas of sourcing and production. Its sustainability ambitions[201] include ten key aspects:

1. Sustainable materials

2. Sustainable packaging

3. Reducing waste

4. CO2 impact

5. Diversity and inclusion

6. Work in local communities

7. Responsible engagement with children

8. Family-friendly workplace

9. Help families through play

10. Responsible supply chain

Revising Goals Can Be Necessary— Being Open about It

The LEGO example about its environmental project shows how important a fully integrated corporate strategy is when it comes to real ambition that is accepted by all stakeholders. When such a bigger cause does exist, identifying—and convincing—soul allies becomes a real opportunity. In 2017, Gavi, the Vaccine Alliance, and Unilever's leading health soap

----

200 https://www.plasticstoday.com/Lego-gets-serious-about-using-more-sustainable-materials

201 https://www.lego.com/de-de/aboutus/sustainability/

brand, Lifebuoy, launched an innovative partnership[202] to protect children under five from childhood illnesses and premature death. By promoting handwashing with soap together with immunization—two of the most cost-effective child survival interventions—the partnership aimed to improve and save many young lives in India. Announced at the World Economic Forum Annual Meeting in Davos, Switzerland, the partnership got support from the government of the Netherlands through Gavi's Matching Fund mechanism and from the government of India, where the initial project to implement a joint approach to promote healthier behaviors took place. India has the highest number of pneumonia and diarrhea deaths among children in the world with nearly 300,000 children dying from these illnesses every year. Lack of handwashing with soap can contribute to such preventable diseases. While progress is being made with the introduction of rotavirus and pneumococcal vaccines, as well as hygiene programs across the world, more needs to be done to accelerate the fight against these diseases. The program's mission was supported by UK Aid and global NGOs such as WaterAid and Save the Children next to intergovernmental organizations (IGOs) like UNICEF and UNHCR—impressive.

Sometimes, ambitions are not realistic, however. Unilever has experienced that. The education program promoting handwashing was supposed to reach one billion children by 2017, but that did not happen. Unilever's Lifebuoy brand was carrying the flag to reduce the incidence of respiratory infection and diarrhea, and the company accepted that the goal was missed—and recommitted itself to deliver against that objective with 2020 as the new target date.[203] Unilever set clearly measurable objectives that it was able to influence, but unable to control. And it has engineered its programs to allow the public to hold the company to account. While it did miss its 2015 target, its response to adjust the

----

202 https://www.unilever.com/news/press-releases/2017/gavi-and-unilever-to-tackle-
     preventable-diseases-and-save-childrens-lives.html

203 https://www.unilever.com/news/press-releases/2017/gavi-and-unilever-to-tackle-
     preventable-diseases-and-save-childrens-lives.html

goalpost might have been viewed as cynical in some quarters, but it was not, nor was it punished by the marketplace. Unilever's problem was not in its execution, but in its ambition, and the marketplace tends to forgive a brand for overreaching.

In 2020 Unilever did indeed hit its target of reaching one billion children. In an interview with Samir Singh, Unilever executive vice president of Global Skin Cleansing, The Drum[204] shared the company's key lessons from the past decade and the relevancy in 2020 of the promise that was set out in 2010—because just when the goal was reached, the COVID-19 pandemic created a further challenge to hygiene, not just in the developing world but across the globe as well. "All the work Lifebuoy is doing to reduce the spread of the outbreak is inspired and driven by the brand's purpose of saving lives and helping people fall ill a little less often," Singh said. Recognizing the true meaning of this purpose meant that the messaging had to focus on handwashing per se, not just using Lifebuoy. This was the first time the company leveraged its communication power beyond its own brand. When a company stays true to its purpose—when it actually builds on a shared purpose and its behavior is that consistent across the world, it is fair to say that this embodies corporate soul. Across the globe, Lifebuoy activated this message: 'wash your hands with soap, not just Lifebuoy, but any soap, even that of our competitors' within 24 hours.

According to the history of Unilever, its cofounder William Lever started selling soap in 1894. His purpose was a simple one. It wasn't to get rich. It was this: to help make cleanliness commonplace and bring hygiene, and thereby health, to the masses—a clear purpose that is shared within Unilever's Lifebuoy business still today.[205] Kartik Chandrasekhar, Lifebuoy's global brand vice president, said, "We genuinely come to work wanting to help people. For us, it's this guiding purpose that motivates us."

----

204   https://www.thedrum.com/news/2020/05/14/inside-lifebuoy-s-mission-get-the-world-handwashing

205   https://www.unilever.com/news/news-and-features/Feature-article/2017/soap-suds-and-saving-lives.html

The history of the brand is rich when it comes to the role it has played during various disease outbreaks, be it in times of cholera in 1893, the spread of the Spanish flu in 1918, the 2003 SARS outbreak, and the H1N1 flu in 2009. Samir Singh said, "We started off in three countries and have now reached 1 billion people in 30-plus countries, making this the largest behavior change program in the world through on-ground programs and communication. Lifebuoy's products and our social responsibility are intrinsically linked. Lifebuoy's purpose is grounded on our social responsibility to keep society protected from infections, and we are doing this by ensuring our products reach the most people as quickly as possible. We believe this is the time for everyone to come together for a bigger cause."[206] Again, this goes beyond CSR—it is a fully integrated corporate business and brand strategy and not "just" communication tactics. Unilever is an ideal example of where many elements really come together: ambition, honesty, true cause, and credibility.

This combination presents the key elements for success in partnerships between corporations like Unilever and NGOs like Gavi. This collaboration serves as a role model for companies across all categories where a shared purpose is brought to life through a shared understanding and shared behaviors to the benefit of all. These are two partners that have become real soul allies.

Sarah Chapman, PhD, director and interim global lead of Corporate Responsibility and Sustainability at Deloitte Canada, summarized the key findings of the 2019 Partnership Conference, and they tie in perfectly to the examples in this chapter:[207] "The most important change we are seeing is the shift in the way companies and nonprofits are working together with a focused effort on mutual impact and benefit, particularly in the context of corporate volunteering. Rather than put pressure on

----

206 https://www.thedrum.com/news/2020/05/14/inside-lifebuoy-s-mission-get-the-world-handwashing

207 https://thepartnershipconference.com/11-corporate-partnership-experts-on-the-most-important-trends-in-2019/

nonprofits to provide volunteer activities for hundreds or thousands of employees on one day, companies and nonprofits must look for new and more meaningful ways to work together. We must ensure any project meets a real community need and is mission-driven, not sacrificing program integrity on both sides. Creating partnerships aligned on mutual benefit is the only way to build long-term, sustainable relationships with maximum community impact."

Soul allies are bringing more to the party than "normal" business partners. The alignment of purpose and values allows a mutual reinforcement of both partners' corporate soul, which creates more strength for both moving forward.

Key thoughts to consider on identifying soul allies

Soul Searching in Action	
✓	Are your corporate partnerships connected to the purpose of your company?
✓	How can you tailor your sponsorships to be purpose-led—globally, regionally, or locally?
✓	Have you integrated your corporate social responsibility activities into your overall strategies?
✓	Which NGOs, CSOs, and IGOs are right for your company to partner with?
✓	Are you clear about the most compelling cause to connect your company with? Does the cause and your product/services and your business strategy contribute to helping achieve one (or more) of the seventeen SDGs?
✓	Can you push the ambition for these programs to a higher level?
✓	Do you allow a transparent view on achieving goals—and revising them when necessary?
✓	Are your colleagues who approve partnership agreements totally familiar with the company's ESG approach?

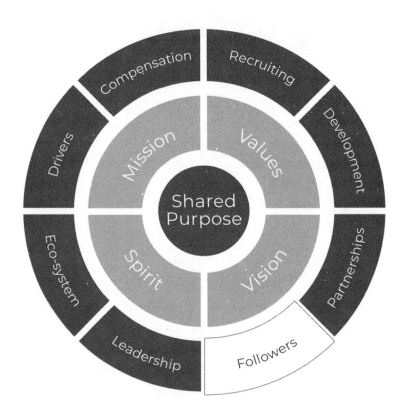

Figure 25: Soul followers as a critical component within the
shared behaviors of the Soul System™.

CHAPTER 12

Create Soul Followers

How can you develop a fan base both internally and externally that
spreads the soul of your company or brand to create a bright future?

Chapter Goal:

Create a family spirit with your stakeholders
and allow disciples to celebrate their passion
and contribute to the soul of the company.

E very year—usually the last Friday before Christmas—a special
gathering happens in Munich. Invitation only. Men and women
meet in a restaurant for a great evening out. The host is Hans
Riedel, the former Porsche executive and Spark44's first chairman, who
calls this gathering "the Annual De-Compression Meeting." It's his way of
saying, "Let's celebrate that we have been able to do great things together
over the years and enjoy our company—even if we are living in different
continents, work in different corporations, or are even retired." That night,
leading executives from more than fifteen global car brands meet—and

all of them have one thing in common: At one point in their career, they crossed Riedel's path. Every now and then when he is late to email the invitations out, he might get some traffic in his inbox: "When are we going to meet in Munich this year?"

The gathering symbolizes the importance of shared values among each of these individuals. Everyone at this gathering is a performance-driven executive, but the importance of joint human interaction unites all of them. Riedel has created a following that is second to none in the category he worked in for decades. Taking a lifetime alumni approach to nurturing relationships with colleagues, as Riedel has done, is a powerful way to create soul followers who help to further strengthen the soul of your company. Here's how Riedel did it.

Shared Experiences Last Forever

Do you remember the bonus payment you received six years ago? Probably not. But if you are being asked, "Do you remember when we launched the Porsche Boxster in Scottsdale, Arizona?" there will be a smile on your face if you were part of the crowd that was on-site. Riedel's mantra has been very straightforward: "We approached our internal and external stakeholders with a unified message—if you join Porsche, you belong to a really appealing community." Building that community has been a key pillar in the success story that created his legacy. A very consistent approach on three levels—employee, dealer, and customer—is the secret behind the success story he created at Porsche. Riedel made sure that three global trends were woven into each and every decision the company took to bring it back on the road to the future:

1. Global sociodemographic development = all people grow older

2. Main human aspiration = everybody wants to feel younger

3. Personal purpose = everybody wants to belong to an attractive community that is bigger than him

With these trends in mind, Porsche ensured that its global employees, dealers, and customers were not just able but wanted to be on the right path. Every time the company called its stakeholders to an international sales conference, you could be sure that those three messages were interpreted in the context of the time. Figure 26 shows the five key themes that always built on one another—and the success in the marketplace that happened in between. These themes gave direction to the company regarding the next milestone in its race to rebuild its glorious reputation. But more than that, beyond very clear and compelling language, they were supported by well-thought-through product initiatives and a solid plan to achieve them. However, the impact of events as such triggered a shared desire, and, equally important, a shared commitment to reach them. In the early phase, these conferences happened annually before Porsche extended the period in between them, but each of these events had the three global trends at their heart.

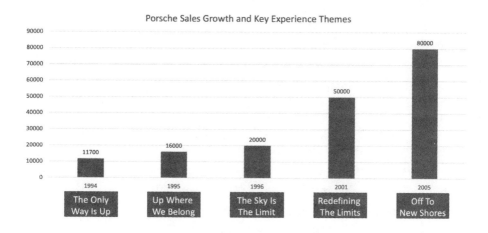

Figure 26: Porsche sales growth and key experience themes.

"These five war cries were critical to how we have been able to steer the business worldwide," remembers Riedel.[208] Every time he invited his global business leaders to a sales conference, he followed the principle laid out by that master of rhetoric, Aristotle: Three things you need to do—tell them what you are going to tell them, tell them, then tell them what you told them. As I noted in chapter 5, this triptych is critical to leaders' credibility, and it certainly served Riedel well—people who joined these conferences remembered what it was that they were supposed to accomplish when they left, and they left with a sense of certainty that the next conversation would be about the status of achievement of these objectives.

If you consider the different situations that Riedel was facing during his tenure at Porsche, this way of presenting information ensured that no one ever forgot what they did together as a team. The power of purpose as EY looks at it is so potent.[209] Referring to past experiences and themes is critical, and so is celebrating the successes and guiding the way to the next summit—you don't climb Mount Everest in just one attempt; you have to be able to climb mountains at much lower levels before you are ready to get to the top. But make no mistake, having clarity about the purpose is mission critical. This is confirmed by the EY report "Why Businesses Must Harness the Power of Purpose,"[210] which was quoted in chapter 3 and which identifies the full integration of purpose into strategic, as well as daily, decisions and actions (shared behaviors) as the critical success factor: "This link between purpose, authenticity and trust is important to emphasize if a company is to improve, not just safeguard, its performance and standing in the eyes of shareholders and society alike. A clear purpose, based on human values—that is authentic and consistent with businesses' actions—is a foundation stone upon which reputation and performance are built."

For Riedel during his time at Porsche, shared experiences were critical to building a community of internal soul followers. He would make

----

208 Hans Riedel, in an interview with the author, 2020.

209, 210 https://www.ey.com/en_gl/purpose/why-business-must-harness-the-power-of-purpose

statements or relate stories decades later that would confirm the impact of those shared experiences. In talking with him, there was one key thought— a red thread—throughout the conversation: "At the end, it is always about people. The human being next to you."[211] And the diversity of an international team that sang from the same song sheet created a bond that allowed the company to move from strength to strength.

Here is what the EY study[212] says about the power of shared purpose: "Purpose can be used to tap into our basic human need to be part of something greater than ourselves—to contribute to a wider group or bigger goal. Purpose can also be harnessed to integrate diverse global teams in new ways, helping them to focus on and reach a common goal—something that's increasingly important as organizations try to deal with disruption."

> "Purpose can be used to tap into our basic human need to be part of something greater than ourselves—to contribute to a wider group or bigger goal."

There has been a common theme of aligning personal purpose and the corporation's purpose in leadership discussions recently. Obviously, that's the cherry on the cake. However, when you look at the reality within the EY study, the objective for any leader is very clear on first sight. These are the percentages of how employees perceive the reality of their company's purpose:

- Our organization's strategy is reflective of our sense of purpose (50%)

- My organization has a strong sense of purpose (46%)

- Our staff has a clear understanding of organizational purpose and commitment to core values/ beliefs (38%)

- - - - - - - - - - - -

211 Hans Riedel, in an interview with the author, 2020.

212 https://www.ey.com/en_gl/purpose/why-business-must-harness-the-power-of-purpose

- Our business model and operations are well aligned with our purpose (37%)

Not a single statement has a higher acceptance rate than 50%; the lowest is at 37%. This is the reality. Companies have a hard time sharing their purpose with their staff and an even harder time creating a shared understanding of what this means to the company and each and every employee. Since actions speak louder than words, the behaviors across the organization are hardly aligned—because they are not shared behaviors but oftentimes more random individual or team behaviors.

Communication is key. With the extreme numbers of messages everybody receives at the workplace day in, day out, ensuring that those messages "land" has never been more critical. In order to "land" them, repetition is a very powerful approach.

"There's no other answer to how to work through disruption than to get a lot of different points of view and be able to listen to them and move those ideas forward," says Nancy A. Altobello, global vice chair of Talent at EY.[213] It is this shared purpose that is the foundation of everything else.

Allow Customers to Become Ambassadors

When my wife and I arrived at a wonderful Relais & Châteaux hotel in the French Jura, we were surprised by the number of Porsche cars that dominated the hotel's car park. It was a group of Porsche drivers from a Porsche Club that enjoyed the late summer days in the French Alps for great scenic drives and a superb hospitality experience. It should not have been a surprise. Upon Riedel joining Porsche, his analysis was pretty clear: "When you buy a Porsche, you buy into a world of experiences and

----

213 https://www.ey.com/en_gl/purpose/why-business-must-harness-the-power-of-purpose

a community that is really aspirational."[214] Back in 1994, there were six hundred Porsche Clubs around the world. They were basically independent groups of passionate drivers who had built connections with one another locally and enjoyed great rides together. He realized that there was an untapped potential for the success of the brand and the company in the years to come—but what was needed was to move from these independent groups to become a community that shared not only the love of the car they were driving, but also to share the values and aspirations of the brand. When Riedel left the firm, that number had grown to 115,000 members. Every year, the presidents of these clubs were invited to join an annual gathering. "These club members were the perfect multipliers for our brand. When we invited them, they were allowed to bring guests—the result: Generations of passionate car enthusiasts found a connection to the brand on a personal level." In other words, the company has been able to create real soul followers, people who identify with the company, the brand, and the product to a degree that they even spend their precious free time celebrating that association. That is priceless.

But getting there was a bumpy ride. Riedel notes there are numerous stories and anecdotes of local Porsche Club presidents who were more committed to their own egos than to the benefit of the community. "We created an identity and a set of values for all clubs to ensure global consistency—that was anything but easy given legal challenges in various countries," he said. "But it was necessary to clean it up in order to give our global strategy a chance to succeed." He recalls that at the end, all were on board. The clubs became a great platform to build a community of like-minded people who became customers for life. Whether it has been special car editions for club members that were quickly sold out, special access to classic cars and required repair services, or great drive experiences—all of these benefits ensured that the loyalty was second to none.

----

214 Hans Riedel, in an interview with the author, 2020.

Deborah Ginsburg from Strategia Design shared her view on the genius behind the program in the company's blog:[215]

> The other day we were talking in the office and Kurt, our Creative Director, shared this picture of his son at a weekend car event. Kurt is a member of PCA (Porsche Club of America) and his son, at a mere 5 years old, is a member of PCA Juniors. In seeing this picture, I was struck by the pure branding genius of Porsche. Here is a child that has been not only exposed to the brand, but has been immersed in a joyful brand experience very early in his life. This young boy is likely to be a Porsche fan for life—and, more importantly (from a business perspective), a future customer. As parents, we enjoy sharing our favorite brands with our kids, and Porsche has made this easy and fun by facilitating a group of young brand enthusiasts. Organizations that can involve both parents and kids help to create memories, connections, and long-term brand love.

Ginsburg believes that there are three key lessons to be learned:

1. Make your best customers feel special.

2. Let your customers contribute to the brand experience.

3. Reward your most loyal customers.

With more than 100,000 members in 144 regional chapters across the United States, the PCA is a real success story. There are a variety of perks for members: social events, tech talks, driver's education events, help with technical problems, and more. What is really impressive is the fact that the club and its activities are not managed by executives from the brand.

- - - - - - - - - - - -

215 https://www.strategiadesign.com/blog/2018/2/16/3-tips-for-creating-a-lifelong-customer-from-porsche

Said Ginsburg, "[The PCA] was created by a fan and the endeavor was happily encouraged by the Porsche corporation. If your customers are eager to contribute to the experience of your brand, provide them the opportunity to do so and reward them for it. It will only make them love you more."

Taking Brand Loyalty to a New Level

In 2020, Porsche operated seven brand experience centers across the world: Atlanta and Los Angeles in the United States, Shanghai in China, Le Mans in France, Silverstone in the United Kingdom, and Leipzig and Hockenheim in Germany. The one in Leipzig is based on the factory compound and offers a direct collection of a newly built vehicle by the owner. More than 30,000 new car buyers make use of that opportunity every year—that is more than 10 percent given a total annual sales volume of 280,000 cars in 2019. If one looks back to the year of the relaunch of the Porsche brand, and actually the entire company in 1994, the results to date are quite impressive as the following figure demonstrates.

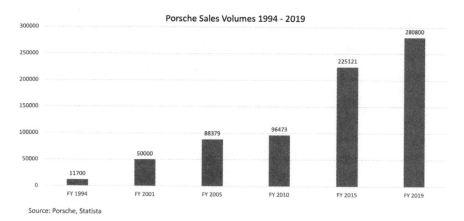

Figure 27: Porsche global sales development, 1994–2019.

These new owners are coming to Leipzig to experience something special—a priceless day at the heart of the brand. They do arrive from all over the world—up to three adults or two adults and two children under eighteen years of age can come on the program. The number of people who can take part in the driving event at Leipzig depends on the vehicle model in question, and customers are asked to plan for approximately five hours for the Factory Collection program.

The whole experience is built around the motto that Riedel established: "The Excitement Company." The Factory Collection website[216] explains that a lot of developments have come about from Porsche's experience on the racetrack—leading to an opportunity to sense the passion for motorsport when cars are handed over in Leipzig. Be it the factory tour, a "dynamic handover" of the new car through an experienced Porsche instructor, or an exhibition of historic and current cars—when you arrive you have already made your decision to buy into the brand. When the roll-up door opens and you leave, chances are high that you fully understood the soul of the company and have become a soul follower for life. These devoted Porsche customers simply feel the heritage, the passion, the excitement: In short, they experience the soul of the brand and the company. On top of that, they enjoy connection to like-minded people around the world who enjoy driving a Porsche wherever it suits them. Like those in the French Alps . . .

A Community of Fans Turns into a Family

The September 2020 issue of the *Porsche Club News*[217] addressed its worldwide members in the midst of the COVID-19 global crisis like this: "The Porsche Clubs are the heart and soul of our worldwide Porsche family. In times when social distancing is mandatory, we still stand together with

----

216   https://www.porsche-leipzig.com/en/offers/factory-collection/factory-collection/
217   https://www.porscheclubnews.com/prod/clubs/clubnews.nsf/content/en-currentissue

the same enthusiasm and even greater unity. Because it's our passion that brings us together, even across the miles—in your Club and in the world-wide Club community."

"The heart and soul" and "worldwide community"—these are terms that you would not expect in the context of a customer association. But it shows how far the program that got a heavy push from Riedel and his colleagues in the mid-1990s has come. In that September 2020 issue, examples of the different approaches of many clubs around the world are showcased, all with the same objective: How can we continue our community life in times of social distancing?

Examples from Mexico, Bosnia and Herzegovina, Belgium, the United States, Hong Kong, Germany, South Africa, Guatemala, Chile, and Singapore—to just name a few—show how close the bond between fellow members as well as between members and the company has become. Juan Pablo Guzman Giraud, president of Porsche Club Mexico, said, "The solidarity among members and the feeling of being part of something bigger have grown even further. And everyone will emerge from the crisis with even more enthusiasm."[218]

The activities that form the Porsche Club Great Britain are considered particularly impressive by the company: "'The heart of our Club is our sense of community, we stick together like a family,' says Edwina Pike. 'We are friends, after all.' And that is why the British Club President and her colleagues have organized countless virtual events, including a 'Pub Quiz' moved to the internet, as well as light-hearted online events with creative titles such as 'Dream Garage,' 'Cayman Clinic,' 'Porsche Night not at Ace Café.' There are also online photography courses where the Club members teach their colleagues how to present their Porsche in photos in the best possible way. 'We hold such virtual events almost every evening,' reports Pike. Club life: 'Stronger than ever before,' she maintains. 'There is a

----

218 https://www.porscheclubnews.com/prod/clubs/clubnews.nsf/content/en-pcn_
      current_202004_community

tremendous feeling of solidarity. We all help each other.' And this also naturally includes support on a private level."

Pretty amazing and a great testimonial for the spirit and purpose[219] of the club—whose purpose, as can be read in the club's founding articles, is "to bring together all Porsche drivers in a spirit of friendship and camaraderie." When the clubs celebrated their sixtieth anniversary in 2012, 640 Porsche Clubs existed around the world with 181,000 club members who "bear witness to the enthusiasm for Porsche and the close connection they feel with the brand and the Porsche company."

Connecting Humans with Humans

Too often, the connection with a company or brand is not a human-to-human interaction. Instead, it feels like a machine-to-human interaction. The principle behind the success of leaders with their internal stakeholders and their external stakeholders, too, is human-to-human interaction. The examples from Hans Riedel show the impact that can happen when strategic clarity and emotional intelligence connect—interactions become effective, connections become stronger, and a loyalty emerges that has the power to drive long-term success, both for the company and its customers.

Corporate soul can become tangible inside and outside the corporation. In the words of social philosopher Charles Handy:[220]

People need leadership.
Things need management.
It is dangerous to get it the other way around.

---

219 content.us.porsche-clubs.porsche.com/porscheclubs/klassieke-porsche-911-en-912-club/
      pc_main.nsf/web/49C0E5562E6F7D23C1257F600036B5E4/$File/60%20Years%20
      History%20Porsche%20clubs%20Part%201%201952%201962.pdf

220 https://www.caplorhorizons.org/updates/why-is-it-the-century-of-leadership

Key thoughts to consider on creating soul followers

Soul Searching in Action	
✓	Have you created a regular set of shared experiences for your associates at different levels?
✓	Are you harnessing your company's shared purpose to integrate diverse global teams?
✓	Do your customers feel like clients—or are they real ambassadors or even disciples?
✓	Which touchpoints can you create to allow disciples to celebrate their passion and contribute to the soul of the company?
✓	Have you created a family spirit with your stakeholders?
✓	Are your interactions just transactions or social encounters that also solve a business need?
✓	Have you put a corporate alumni program in place?

The Bookends of My Professional Career

"In a rapidly changing world, how we do things has never been more important. Our core values guide everything we do. Strong individually, it is how Creativity & Entrepreneurship work together that makes them powerful and true to our culture of participation and partnership."[221] This is how publishing giant Bertelsmann defines its essentials today. When I started my professional career in the early 1980s at that very company, I was confronted with similar words by entrepreneur Reinhard Mohn, who set the path to growth for a small publishing company in Germany to become a world-leading media house. He had developed a sound leadership philosophy that guided the media conglomerate through the decades ahead. This is where I first learned

- - - - - - - - - - -

221 https://www.bertelsmann.de/media/verantwortung/downloads/englisch/bertelsmann-essentials-eng.pdf

about the principle of participation and partnership—and this is what has remained stuck in my mind since then. What I did not know at the age of twenty-three was that the definition of culture was the actual foundation that allowed the company to become what it had been famous for at that time and now again. It was also the first time I heard that term "he is the *soul* of the company" in the hallways.

In August 2019, Ranjay Gulati, the head of the organizational behavioral unit at Harvard Business School, published an article in *Harvard Business Review* titled "The Soul of a Start-Up."[222] His analysis of the energy and soul in start-ups is summed up with the words "Most founders believe their start-ups are about more than their business models."

This mirrors my own experience, since we as the management team at Spark44 had worked long and hard to establish that "more" that ended up in the galvanizing thought of "We empower people to challenge conventions so that amazing things happen." That is what we had been doing from day one until the day I left, and it did wonders in the commitment of our people and the quality of the output of our work. Amazing things happened.

- - - - - - - - - - - -

222 https://hbr.org/2019/07/the-soul-of-a-start-up

The Definitions and Questions You Need to Ask

I n short, *purpose* declares why the company exists, *vision* defines the desired future state, *mission* expresses the direction that is required to make the purpose become real, *values* characterize all behaviors, and *spirit* embodies the corporate culture.

Purpose

In my view, Gallup[1] has come up with the best definition: "At its core, a company's purpose is a bold affirmation of its reason for being in business. It conveys what the organization stands for in historical, ethical, emotional and practical terms. No matter how it's communicated to employees and customers, a company's purpose is the driving force that enables a company to define its true brand and create its desired culture."

---

1   https://www.gallup.com/workplace/236573/company-purpose-lot-words.aspx

Achieving clarity in this area is critical. Katrina Marshall Dyrting has identified key questions that help to get to the better purpose statements:[2]

- Why does our organization's existence matter?

- Why are we important to the people we serve?

- Why would anyone dedicate their time and passion to our company?

- What would be lost in the world if we no longer existed?

She also suggests to make sure that the purpose statement is as follows:

- Inspiring to those inside the company

- Inspiring to your key stakeholders

- Something that's as valid 100 years from now as it is today

- A statement that helps you see possibilities about what you *could* do

- Truly authentic to your company

Vision

Wikipedia[3] provides a clear definition: "A vision statement is an inspirational statement of an idealistic emotional future of a company or group. A vision statement provides direction, it sets a course toward a future that tells the people in that organization what the group believes, how to behave, and what kinds of decisions to make without explicitly doing so. As a result, a vision—to have vision—means to imagine a world that does not yet exist and intends to inspire people to make it a reality."

---

2   https://medium.com/agileforreal/wyt-december-edition-finding-your-organisational-purpose-2ea70cff5625

3   https://en.wikipedia.org/wiki/Vision_statement

In my words, it is a guide for management to ensure that any strategic decisions are in sync with the long-term view for the company.

Again, Katrina Marshall Dyrting has identified key questions that help to get to the better purpose statements:[4]

- What do we aspire to be?

- What do we hope to achieve in the future?

- What will our impact be?

Mission

Also, here the Wikipedia definition of a mission statement is straightforward: "It is a short statement of why an organization exists, what its overall goal is, identifying the goal of its operations: what kind of product or service it provides, its primary customers or market, and its geographical region of operation."

In this area, Dyrting's key questions help to get to better mission statements:[5]

- How will we get there?

- What do we focus on along the way?

- What is our core business?

Values

The leading employee communications and advocacy platform Smarp[6] has a very compelling definition: "In essence, your company values are the beliefs, philosophies, and principles that drive your business. They impact

---

the employee experience you deliver as well as the relationship you develop with your customers, partners, and shareholders."

As with all other elements of shared understanding, it is critical to be very specific. Too many corporate values sound the same within the category the business is in. My recommendation is this: Don't be afraid to be crystal clear. It pays off when all stakeholders experience the values written on the office walls in the real behaviors of your actions.

In my experience, getting to better value statements is an interesting exercise—often, it helps to start by asking which behaviors you do not want to tolerate inside your company. Above all, they must be easy to understand and—for international companies—stand the cross-border cultural check:

- Are we clear about the desired behaviors?
- Do they characterize life at our company?
- Are we avoiding category jargon?
- Will they be emotionally embraced by our people?

Spirit

There is no prevailing definition of *spirit* in the corporate world. Here is my definition: When purpose, vision, mission, and values are in sync, a unique spirit will emerge within the company. Corporate spirit fuels the behaviors inside the company that allow it to create a powerful identity that everyone immediately feels—customers and prospects alike. It defines the culture of the firm in all its aspects—for better or worse.

Spirit can become an irresistible source of power for any company. It complements the ecosystem of the elements of shared understanding (vision, mission, values) centered on a shared purpose, allowing for shared behaviors to develop corporate soul.

But spirit is nothing that you can define in statements like purpose, vision, mission, and values; hence, having key questions is not adequate in my view. The following questions are rather a mirror to the corporate culture that companies should hold up regularly to understand whether the corporate spirit is in sync with purpose, vision, mission, and values:

- Does our employee survey show significant year-on-year deviations?

- Do our customers recognize the spirit of our company; do we measure it?

- Does our employer brand reflect the spirit—and is it attractive enough?

Appendix

Hilton: A Case Study of Building Corporate Soul

Hilton operates by five key behaviors that are known to everyone in the company:

1.	**Trust** Builds strong trust with all or nearly all of its employees, regardless of personal backgrounds or role
2.	**Goals** Consistently reinforces the company's larger vision and goals, and connects individuals to them in personally meaningful ways
3.	**Development** Drives a continuous improvement and learning mindset by investing in mentoring and development of others
4.	**Recognition** Celebrates successes of teams and individuals without seeking personal credit
5.	**Relationships** Cultivates strong connections and relationships both within and across teams across the organization

Table 11: Hilton's five key behaviors for leaders.

These leadership behaviors ensure that the company's six core values are not just a PowerPoint slide, but are also constantly reinforced by the everyday actions of Hilton's worldwide staff.

1.	**Hospitality**	We're passionate about delivering exceptional guest experiences.
2.	**Integrity**	We do the right thing, all the time.
3.	**Leadership**	We're leaders in our industry and in our communities.
4.	**Teamwork**	We're team players in everything we do.
5.	**Ownership**	We're the owner of our actions and decisions.
6.	**Now**	We operate with a sense of urgency and discipline.

Table 12: Hilton's six core values.

In 2018, Great Place to Work® ranked Hilton as its number one company and compiled a thorough case study on what makes the company such a "great place to work" (I reference this study in the book). The case study confirmed that Hilton is maximizing the human potential of its people at industry-leading levels, which enables increasing profitability and strong stock market performance. The study also reported that Hilton's culture ("For All" culture in the Great Place to Work® terminology) offered important lessons for organizations of any industry in how to treat their employees just as well as their customers.

Airbnb CEO Brian Chesky's Email about COVID-19 Layoffs

I excerpted portions from this email in chapter 4 as part of my discussion of the incredible understanding that Brian Chesky has for the soul of his company. But I'm including the email in its entirety here because it is one of the most profound statements that embody corporate soul in times of crisis that I have ever read:[1]

A Message from Airbnb Co-Founder
and CEO Brian Chesky

May 5, 2020

Earlier today, Airbnb Co-Founder and CEO Brian Chesky sent the following note to Airbnb employees.

This is my seventh time talking to you from my house. Each time we've talked, I've shared good news and bad news, but today I have to share some very sad news.

When you've asked me about layoffs, I've said that nothing is off the table.

Today, I must confirm that we are reducing the size of the Airbnb workforce. For a company like us whose mission is centered around belonging, this is incredibly difficult to confront, and it will be even harder for those who have to leave Airbnb. I am going to share as many details as I can on how I arrived at this decision, what we are doing for those leaving, and what will happen next.

Let me start with how we arrived at this decision. We are collectively living through the most harrowing crisis of our lifetime, and as it began to unfold, global travel came to a standstill. Airbnb's business has been hit hard, with revenue this year forecasted to be less than half of what we earned in 2019. In

---

1   https://news.airbnb.com/a-message-from-co-founder-and-ceo-brian-chesky/

response, we raised $2 billion in capital and dramatically cut costs that touched nearly every corner of Airbnb.

While these actions were necessary, it became clear that we would have to go further when we faced two hard truths: We don't know exactly when travel will return. When travel does return, it will look different.

While we know Airbnb's business will fully recover, the changes it will undergo are not temporary or short-lived. Because of this, we need to make more fundamental changes to Airbnb by reducing the size of our workforce around a more focused business strategy.

Out of our 7,500 Airbnb employees, nearly 1,900 teammates will have to leave Airbnb, comprising around 25% of our company. Since we cannot afford to do everything that we used to, these cuts had to be mapped to a more focused business.

Travel in this new world will look different, and we need to evolve Airbnb accordingly. People will want options that are closer to home, safer, and more affordable. But people will also yearn for something that feels like it's been taken away from them—human connection. When we started Airbnb, it was about belonging and connection. This crisis has sharpened our focus to get back to our roots, back to the basics, back to what is truly special about Airbnb—everyday people who host their homes and offer experiences.

This means that we will need to reduce our investment in activities that do not directly support the core of our host community. We are pausing our efforts in Transportation and Airbnb Studios, and we have to scale back our investments in Hotels and Lux.

These decisions are not a reflection of the work from people on these teams, and it does not mean everyone on these teams will be leaving us. Additionally, teams across all of Airbnb will be impacted. Many teams will be reduced in size based on how well they map to where Airbnb is headed.

How we approached reductions

It was important that we had a clear set of principles, guided by our core values, for how we would approach reductions in our workforce. These were our guiding principles:

- Map all reductions to our future business strategy and the capabilities we will need.

- Do as much as we can for those who are impacted.

- Be unwavering in our commitment to diversity.

- Optimize for 1:1 communication for those impacted.

- Wait to communicate any decisions until all details are landed—transparency of only partial information can make matters worse.

- I have done my best to stay true to these principles.

Process for making reductions

Our process started with creating a more focused business strategy built on a sustainable cost model. We assessed how each team mapped to our new strategy, and we determined the size and shape of each team going forward. We then did a comprehensive review of every team member and made decisions based on critical skills, and how well those skills matched our future business needs.

The result is that we will have to part with teammates that we love and value. We have great people leaving Airbnb, and other companies will be lucky to have them.

To take care of those that are leaving, we have looked across severance, equity, healthcare, and job support and done our best to treat everyone in a compassionate and thoughtful way.

Severance

Employees in the US will receive 14 weeks of base pay, plus one additional week for every year at Airbnb. Tenure will be rounded to the nearest year. For example, if someone has been at Airbnb for 3 years and 7 months, they will get an additional 4 weeks of salary, or 18 weeks of total pay. Outside the US, all employees will receive at least 14 weeks of pay, plus tenure increases consistent with their country-specific practices.

Equity

We are dropping the one-year cliff on equity for everyone we've hired in the past year so that everyone departing, regardless of how long they have been here, is a shareholder. Additionally, everyone leaving is eligible for the May 25 vesting date.

Healthcare

In the midst of a global health crisis of unknown duration, we want to limit the burden of healthcare costs. In the US, we will cover 12 months of health insurance through COBRA. In all other countries, we will cover health insurance costs through the end of 2020. This is because we're either legally unable to continue coverage, or our current plans will not allow for an extension. We will also provide four months of mental health support through Konterra.

Job support

Our goal is to connect our teammates leaving Airbnb with new job opportunities. Here are five ways we can help:

- Alumni Talent Directory—We will be launching a public-facing website to help teammates leaving find new jobs. Departing employees can opt-in to have profiles, resumes, and work samples accessible to potential employers.

- Alumni Placement Team—For the remainder of 2020, a significant portion of Airbnb Recruiting will become an Alumni Placement Team. Recruiters that are staying with Airbnb will provide support to departing employees to help them find their next job.

- RiseSmart—We are offering four months of career services through RiseSmart, a company that specializes in career transition and job placement services.

- Employee Offered Alumni Support—We are encouraging all remaining employees to opt-in to a program to assist departing teammates find their next role.

- Laptops—A computer is an important tool to find new work, so we are allowing everyone leaving to keep their Apple laptops.

Here is what will happen next

I want to provide clarity to all of you as soon as possible. We have employees in 24 countries, and the time it will take to provide clarity will vary based on local laws and practices. Some countries require notifications about employment to be received in a very specific way. While our process may differ by country, we have tried to be thoughtful in planning for every employee.

In the US and Canada, I can provide immediate clarity. Within the next few hours, those of you leaving Airbnb will receive a calendar invite to a departure meeting with a senior leader in your department. It was important to us that wherever we legally could, people were informed in a personal, 1:1 conversation. The final working day for departing employees based in the US and Canada will be Monday, May 11. We felt Monday would give people time to begin taking next steps and say goodbye—we understand and respect how important this is.

Some employees who are staying will have a new role, and will receive a meeting invite with the subject "New Role" to learn more about it. For those of you in the US and Canada who are staying on the Airbnb team, you will not receive a calendar invite.

At 6pm pacific time, I will host a world@ meeting for our Asia-Pacific teams. At 12am pacific time, I will host a world@ meeting for our Europe and Middle East teams. Following each of these meetings, we'll proceed with next steps in each country based on local practices.

I've asked all Airbnb leaders to wait to bring their teams together until the end of this week out of respect to our teammates being impacted. I want to give everyone the next few days to process this, and I'll host a CEO Q&A again this Thursday at 4pm pacific time.

Some final words

As I have learned these past eight weeks, a crisis brings you clarity about what is truly important. Though we have been through a whirlwind, some things are more clear to me than ever before.

First, I am thankful for everyone here at Airbnb. Throughout this harrowing experience, I have been inspired by all of you. Even in the worst of circumstances, I've seen the very best of us. The world needs human connection now more than ever, and I know that Airbnb will rise to the occasion. I believe this because I believe in you.

Second, I have a deep feeling of love for all of you. Our mission is not merely about travel. When we started Airbnb, our original tagline was, "Travel like a human." The human part was always more important than the travel part. What we are about is belonging, and at the center of belonging is love.

To those of you staying, one of the most important ways we can honor those who are leaving is for them to know that their contributions mattered, and that they will always be part of Airbnb's story. I am confident their work will live on, just like this mission will live on.

To those leaving Airbnb, I am truly sorry. Please know this is not your fault. The world will never stop seeking the qualities and talents that you brought to Airbnb . . . that helped make Airbnb. I want to thank you, from the bottom of my heart, for sharing them with us.

Brian

Ikea's Values

The Swedish retailer is a classic example of a company that forms meaningful partnerships based on its core values as explained in chapter 11. The description of these values in my mind is a perfect example of how to write values for a company: They are clear and easy to understand. At the same time they avoid any jargon and are in the best sense straightforward:

1. **Togetherness**

   Togetherness is at the heart of the IKEA culture. We are strongest when we trust each other, pull in the same direction, and have fun together.

2. **Caring for people and planet**

   We want to be a force for positive change. We have the possibility to make a significant and lasting impact—today and for the generations to come.

3. **Cost-consciousness**

   As many people as possible should be able to afford a beautiful and functional home. We constantly challenge ourselves and others to make more from less without compromising on quality.

4. **Simplicity**

   A simple, straightforward, and down-to-earth way of being is part of our Smålandic heritage. It is about being ourselves and staying close to reality. We are informal, pragmatic, and see bureaucracy as our biggest enemy.

5. **Renew and improve**

   We are constantly looking for new and better ways forward. Whatever we are doing today, we can do better tomorrow. Finding solutions to almost impossible challenges is part of our success and a source of inspiration to move on to the next challenge.

6. **Different with a meaning**

   We are not like other companies and we don't want to be. We like to question existing solutions, think in unconventional ways, experiment, and dare to make mistakes—always for a good reason.

7. **Give and take responsibility**

   We believe in empowering people. Giving and taking responsibility are ways to grow and develop as individuals. Trusting each other, being positive and forward-looking, inspires everyone to contribute to development.

8. **Lead by example**

   We see leadership as an action, not a position. We look for people's values before competence and experience. People who "walk the talk" and lead by example. It is about being our best self and bringing out the best in in each other.

Larry Fink's 2019 Letter to CEOs. https://www.blackrock.com/americas-offshore/en/2019-larry-fink-ceo-letter. Copyright © 2019 Black Rock, Inc. All rights reserved. Reproduced by permission.

From "Business Roundtable Redefines the Purpose of a Corporation to Promote 'An Economy That Serves All Americans.'" https://www.businessroundtable.org/business-roundtable-redefines-the-purpose-of-a-corporation-to-promote-an-economy-that-serves-all-americans Copyright © Business Roundtable. Reproduced by permission.

Alex Gorsky's Farewell Letter. Copyright © Johnson & Johnson Services, Inc.. All rights reserved.

From "Every year we throw away the trophies and start all over again," from Egon Zehnder. July 31, 2015. Interview with Jørgen Vig Knudstorp. https://www.egonzehnder.com/what-we-do/leadership-solutions/organizational-transformation/insights/every-year-we-throw-away-the-trophies-and-start-all-over-again. Copyright © 2015 Egon Zehnder.

From "2021 Global RepTrak 100" Report. https://ri.reptrak.com/2021-globalreptrak-100-reputation-download-report/download-now. Copyright © 2021 The RepTrak™ Company.

"A Message from Co-Founder and CEO Brian Chesky," Airbnb. May 5, 2020. https://news.airbnb.com/a-message-from-co-founder-and-ceo-brian-chesky/ Copyright © 2020 by Airbnb, Inc. Reproduced by permission of Airbnb, Inc. All rights reserved.

The following are reproduced by permission of Glassdoor. Copyright © by Glassdoor. All rights reserved:

Big Nine Values. https://www.glassdoor.com/research/app/uploads/sites/2/2019/06/Measuring-Culture-Final-2.pdf

Donald Sull "The Five Myths of Corporate Culture" https://www.youtube.com/watch?v=q7F4AxyGDAA Interview with Matthew Schuyler. June 23, 2017. https://www.glassdoor.com/employers/blog/how-hilton-manages-its-global-enterprise-for-great-leadership/ Graphic "The Workplace Factors that Matter Most to Employee Satisfaction in the US." https://www.glassdoor.com/research/employee-satisfaction-drivers/#

From "Uncomfortable Conversations: The Importance of Black Mentorship" by Lindsay Rittenhouse, *AdAge*, July 8, 2020. Copyright © 2020 by Crain Communications. Reproduced by permission.

"How You Promote People Can Make or Break Company Culture" by Chinwe Onyeagoro, Jessica Rohman, Michael C. Bush, from *Harvard Business Review*, January 2018. Copyright © 2018 by *Harvard Business Review*. Reproduced by permission. All rights reserved. hbr.org.

From "Purpose Shifting from Why to How." April 22, 2020/Article https://www.mckinsey.com/business-functions/organization/our-insights/purpose-shifting-from-why-to-how. Table from "Embedding purpose: fewer slogans, more action. https://www.mckinsey.com/business-functions/strategy-and-corporate-finance/our-insights/the-strategy-and-corporate-finance-blog/embedding-purpose-fewer-slogans-more-action. Copyright © 2020 by McKinsey & Company. Reproduced by permission.

From "A New Framework for Executive Compensation" by Seymour Burchman, *Harvard Business Review*. February 2020. Copyright © 2020 by Harvard Business Publishing. Reproduced by permission. All rights reserved. hbr.org.

From "Your Company Culture Is Who You Hire, Fire, and Promote" by Dr. Cameron Sepah from Medium.com. March 3, 2017. https://medium.com/agileforreal/wyt-december-edition-finding-your-organisational-purpose-2ea70cff5625. Copyright © 2017 by Dr. Cameron Sepah. Used by permission of the author.

From web article "How to Hire for Emotional Intelligence" by Annie McKee from *Harvard Business Review*, February 2016. Copyright © 2016 by Harvard Business Publishing. Reproduced by permission. All rights reserved. hbr.org

"Build a Career Worth Having" by Nathaniel Koloc from *Harvard Business Review*. August 2013. Copyright © 2013 by *Harvard Business Review*. Reproduced by permission. All rights reserved. hbr.org.

"A Letter from Our Founder, Yvon Chouinard," April 22, 2020, from 1% Percent for the Planet. https://www.onepercentfortheplanet.org/stories/a-letter-from-yvon-chouinard. Copyright © 2020 1% for the Planet®. Reproduced by permission.

Index

Figures and tables are indicated by an italicized *f* or *t* following a page number.

A

D

E

Acknowledgments

When I embarked on the journey to write *Building Corporate Soul*, I shared the idea with my longtime friend Kevin Allen. During our mutual collaboration while both of us worked at McCann-Erickson and later on when he supported the success of Spark44, one thing remained: His view did count. This time, his enthusiasm had no limit: "You are really onto something here!" were his words that encouraged me when I shared the initial idea with him. His instinct was correct—whenever I shared the idea with others, they confirmed his view. So, I continued.

At one point Neil Cassie, who wrote the foreword, got involved. We had become friends over a shared view on corporate culture and what it takes to make it aspirational. When I told him about the theme of this book, he volunteered to read the chapters as I wrote them and to offer feedback in parallel. This was very helpful, and I can't thank him enough for the passion he cultivated during the many months of developing this book. He also connected me with Jack Bleakley, a very talented art student at St. Martin's in London. Jack embraced the challenge to create a graphic treatment for the Soul System™, which is featured in this book and has inspired the cover graphics.

On a warm summer afternoon when everyone was under the impression of a certain relief to the constraints that the COVID-19 pandemic had on all of us, I met with my former colleague Lutz Meyer—a seasoned public relations expert who focuses on the ESG facets of building reputation for corporations. His reaction was also very positive, and he volunteered to proofread what I had written. He probably did not know what he was getting himself into. A few weeks after I sent him the manuscript, I received an email saying, "Here comes the first half," and a few weeks later the second part arrived. Knowing Lutz as a not-so-easy-to-convince person, I was impressed by the effort he had put into it and the wisdom he was able to provide. All his comments proved valuable and enriched chapter 11 significantly.

Last but not least, without my son Ivo, I would not have been able to build the analysis to establish the 2021 Soul Index. Thanks to his Excel knowledge, managing the data became easier than I thought. Without these five fine gentlemen, *Building Corporate Soul* would not be what it is that you hold in your hands. To get it there, I have to thank Fast Company Press and the team at Greenleaf Book Group—Justin Branch, Tyler LeBleu, Corrin Foster, Scott James, Sally Garland, Neil Gonzalez, Jeffrey Curry, and Steve Elizalde, who all provided unbelievable support to turn my manuscript into a "real" book.

I especially want to thank Judy Marchman, who had the patience to edit this book. She put herself in the position of an educated reader—oh boy, did she do an amazing job. Basically, she got me to strengthen every argument made in this book. It was quite a ride, but it has been worth every sentence.

About the Author

Ralf Specht is a visionary business leader and creator of the Soul System™, a framework that aligns value-creating employee action with broader corporate strategy through shared understanding and shared purpose. As a founding partner of Spark44, he was the architect of an innovative, industry-first joint venture with Jaguar Land Rover which grew under his leadership to a global revenue of $100+m and 1,200 employees. Previously, he consulted with global companies and brands for more than two decades with McCann Erickson. He is the author of *Building Corporate Soul: Powering Culture & Success with the Soul System™* from Fast Company Press, and the forthcoming *Beyond the Startup: Sparking Operational Innovations for Global Growth*. His driving vision is to make soulless companies a thing of the past.

If you want to get an inside view of Ralf's leadership experience in building Spark44 and growing it from four offices and a team of eighty to nineteen offices and a team of twelve hundred in just a few years, then *Beyond the Startup: Sparking Operational Innovations for Global Growth* is a "must read."

The greatest challenge of any startup and growth company is the transition from an early-stage startup to a robust organization complete with a driving culture, contemporary leadership, organizational infrastructure, and twenty-first-century operating methodologies. In the high interest topic of startups focused on the beginning stages of entrepreneurship, *Beyond the Startup* fills a void in the entrepreneurial discussion on how to scale a second stage startup, laying out in practical terms the tools and practices that made Spark44 a global powerhouse before it joined forces with Accenture Interactive.

Radius Book Group (May 2022)
Hardcover ISBN: 978-1-63576-900-5
eBook ISBN: 978-1-63576-901-2
Also available everywhere digital audiobooks are sold